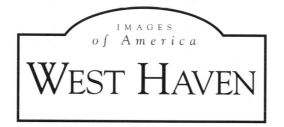

IMAGES
of America

WEST HAVEN

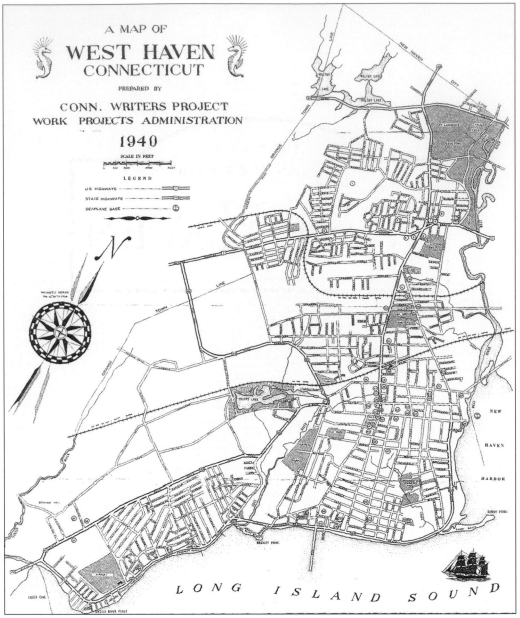

This map was published in the definitive *History of West Haven, Connecticut*, by the Connecticut Writers' Project of the Work Projects Administration, 1940. A major contributor was Harry I. Thompson (1840–1906), West Haven postmaster from 1861 to 1864 and publisher of the *West Haven Journal* from 1873 to 1877.

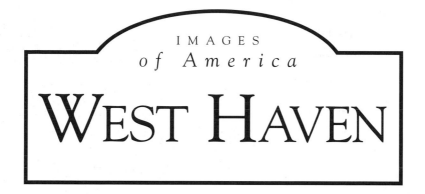

IMAGES

of America

WEST HAVEN

West Haven Historical Society

Published by Arcadia Publishing
Charleston SC, Chicago IL, Portsmouth NH, San Francisco CA

Printed in Great Britain

Library of Congress Catalog Card Number: 2005931044

For all general information contact Arcadia Publishing at:
Telephone 843-853-2070
Fax 843-853-0044
E-mail sales@arcadiapublishing.com
For customer service and orders:
Toll-Free 1-888-313-2665

Visit us on the Internet at http://www.arcadiapublishing.com

CONTENTS

ACKNOWLEDGMENTS

The compilation of this photo-journal history of West Haven was truly a cooperative effort of the trustees, officers, and members of the West Haven Historical Society. My role as researcher and writer was certainly made easier by their diligence, enthusiasm, and endless information. The project gives new meaning to the term human resources. I would particularly like to thank Alice Butler and Ted Wolfe for sharing their wealth of knowledge and their extensive private collections; Mary Head, Bernice Kaercher, Bill Barr, Dr. Jon Purmont, Dan Shine, Jane Dexter, and the members of Annawon Lodge, who provided cards, photographs, memorabilia, and historical data; Betty Roy and Rosemary Roy, who acted as research assistants in the society and library archives; Ceren Laydon for her technical support and computer graphic input; and my mentors, city historians and society past presidents Harriet C. North and Bennett W. Dorman, who encouraged me in my endeavors over the years.

Our intention was to select images, some familiar and many unusual, that touch upon the story of West Haven, its people, businesses, expansion, and uniqueness. We are so very aware of the many facets of the community we could not cover because of limited space and abundance of materials, but we do look forward to compiling a second book.

This book is written in celebration of the 50th anniversary of the founding of the West Haven Historical Society and as part of our outreach and education program. We welcome any photographs, memorabilia, genealogies, or general information and items related to the history of the city for our archives.

—Carole A. Laydon McElrath

INTRODUCTION

West Haven is strategically located on the western shore of New Haven Harbor in south central Connecticut. From its pristine four mile shore one can see the contour of Long Island, a natural barrier, 20 miles to the south. The deep harbor and beaches are somewhat protected by the "Breakwaters," a series of stone walls constructed in the 1880s. This location has been both a blessing and a bane throughout our history.

Long before the first six families crossed the West River from the New Haven Colony, the Podunk, Shagdicoke, and Tunxis tribes summered in the area. The abundance of wildlife in the densely forested region, fertile soil, and fresh water from three tributaries offered a protected natural habitat. Saltwater fish, clams, and mollusks were readily available, as were the oysters from the beds which they maintained. Dutch explorers noted tall white shell mounds along the shoreline long before the Puritan colony was established. Encampments were set up along Old Creek near the sand bar, on the Green and as far from the ocean as Maltby Lakes. Arrowheads and other artifacts may be found throughout the city, often in one's own backyard.

Our history is inextricably tied to that of our neighboring towns: West Farms, with its first six settling families of gentlemen farmers (1648) was an extension of New Haven, and then of the Borough of Orange. West Haven had its own leadership, economic development and tax base, and by 1892 it was necessary to expand beyond the small offices in the Thompson building into a town hall. Twenty-eight years later, in 1921, the town of West Haven became an independent entity, and in 1961 the city of West Haven was incorporated. As the city expanded, neighborhoods were referred to by their local identity such as Prospect Beach, West Shore, and Oyster River. Perhaps the only section which has a specific identification is Allingtown, named after its founders. It is the site of a significant historic event where British Adjutant William Campbell was mortally wounded, tended to by the local ladies, and buried on the Alling and Prudden property. Surrounding Allingtown's small center Green have been two movie theaters, furniture stores, pharmacies, a school which now serves as a senior center, and branch library. It can boast of the highest point in West Haven on Burwell Hill, adjacent to the University of New Haven.

The focus of the early settlers was on the center of the city, and they established the Congregational Meeting House where all vital statistics, tax, and town business records were kept. An early school was established based on the beliefs of the founders of the parent colony, and the first library in the state was opened. In a move which shook the very depths of the New England colonies, ministers from that church united with Yale College leaders in the early 1700s to establish an Anglican Church in West Haven.

Our city's seal, designed by local attorney, teacher and town official Jerome Jermain in 1935, bears the image of militiaman Thomas Painter as he spied the invading British ships entering the harbor. Painter, considered our Paul Revere, consequently raised the alarm in the early hours on July 5, 1779. One thousand, five hundred British and Hessian troops marched through the town on their way to burn New Haven. The history of West Haven cannot be told without recalling the "Williston incident" and British Adjutant Campbell's merciful deed. Through the early years there was a degree of strife as colonials distrusted the loyalists in the town to the point where it is recorded that a gentleman from Oyster River shot his British sympathizer neighbor in the leg for his leanings. Other sympathizers provided beef and fresh produce for British ships during another landing on our shore.

Shipbuilding, seafaring, trade, whalers, and privateers were also part of our history. Many streets are named for the captains, masters and ship owners who brought great wealth and recognition to the community. Their gracious and elegant homes, one of which is a museum today, were testimony to their generations of success. Entrepreneur George Kelsey brought about some dramatic changes when he built his Buckle Shops and extended the local rail line to the shore. His already successful manufacturing plants were in high production with the advent of the Civil War; clamps, rings, and other products for prostheses were in great demand. Along the shoreline and extending through the farmlands were the homeowners involved in the active Underground Railroad; their tunnels and hideaways are known today.

It wasn't long before other large manufacturing plants were built, such as the Mathushek Piano factory which covered an area approximately two square city blocks. The records of the Philadelphia Exposition of 1876, from which we acquired the Connecticut House, note that the piano on exhibit is from a factory in New Haven, but the names of all West Haven residents in attendance were meticulously recorded. The introduction of the expanded rail (trolley) line by the ambitious and creative Kelsey led to the development of the shoreline and a Victorian "White City." Sophisticated travelers enjoyed the genteel amusement park, and the new hotels and inns. Large landowners broke up properties and lured people to town promising a country atmosphere but with the convenience of the trolley.

Police and fire departments grew and fraternal. Social and civic organizations flourished; World War I took its toll. The population again increased in 1921 when families thought it advantageous to move to the new town. Shipyards were eventually converted to the manufacturing of sea planes and power boats; tire manufacturing became a major asset, especially during the second World War. The economic development trend of the 1950s and 1960s made a huge impact as the old Savin Rock Amusement Park was demolished and the beaches were enhanced. As with most towns in the state, large scale manufacturing is non-existent; shopping malls eliminated most independent retailers.

Through all of the changes, West Haven has retained its unique personality. Tens of thousands of people enjoy the summer and fall festivals, dancing and concerts at the beach, great restaurants, farmers' markets, or just walking the three mile pristine shoreline with its monuments and markers. We encourage our readers to visit the aforementioned house museum, the Learning Center for Local History, the Savin Rock (Amusement Park) Museum, or to take the Historical Society's trolley "Tour of Historic West Haven" to learn more about the history of West Haven.

—West Haven Historical Society

One

THE SETTLERS' GREEN

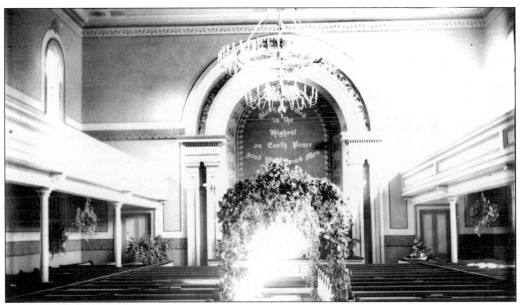

The First Congregational Church of West Haven, a classic example of fine New England architecture, is the pivotal center of the historic district. In this photograph from around 1891, the simple design of the interior is adorned with hanging plants and a bower of fresh flowers for a special occasion.

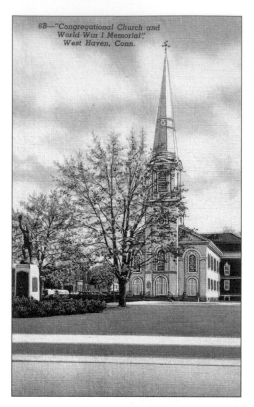

6B—"Congregational Church and World War I Memorial," West Haven, Conn.

The most attractive feature in the city center is West Haven Green, with its First Congregational Church. The original building, a meetinghouse for worship and civic functions, was used for 134 years. It was built on marshy property donated by Samuel Candee and Shubael Painter. A church was erected in 1851, destroyed by fire in 1859, and replaced by the current building in 1860. The Green was deeded to the Borough of West Haven in March 1876.

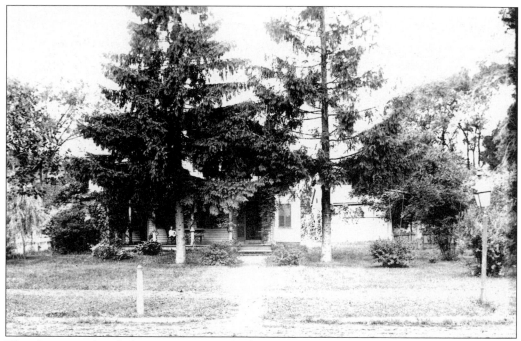

The front porch of the Congregational church parsonage on Savin Avenue offered an advantageous view of the activities in town in the late 1800s.

We the Subscribers Wishing to Subserve and advance
the Interests of Religion & Learning, and being fully
persuaded that a Choice Collection of the best Authers
on Geography, History the belle Letters Divinity and
other Branches of Science may subserve those Interests
and being confident that We ourselves, our Children and
unborn Generations may recieve much Pleasure & Literary
Improvement by frequent Converse with such Authers
and be assisted in maturer Progress in divine Knowledge, We think
it our indispensible Duty to unite in purchasing
such a Collection and forming a Library, to be under
the Direction of those We shall appoint to the Office
of Librarians, And We solemnly Covenant & promise
that We will advance the Sum or Sums set against our
respective Names & be Subject to the Rules & Laws
We shall Ordain in our Metings legally warned; and
that We will Honestly endeavour that the Benevolent Designe of Instituting a Library may be most
fully carryed into Execution ———

    In witness whereof We have hereto set our Names

        Nathan Smith   Noah Williston

    Pr? Joseph Harwin?   Jas Kimberly

    Benjamin Smith   Jeremiah Smith

                 Nathaniel Smith

                 Gilead Kimberly

                 Sam Rand

                 Tho Painter

                 Joseph Smith

                 Nehemiah Kimberly

                 Philemon Smith

                 Nathaniel Davis

                 George Bird

Within 13 years of the British invasion of West Haven on July 5, 1779, local citizens, led by Thomas Painter and Noah Williston, united to form the first public library in the state of Connecticut. The library was housed in the meetinghouse.

Westhaven Library   *Newhaven 5:ᵗʰ Octᵒ: 1792*

Bot of Isaac Beers

1 Davies.. Sermons — 3 Vols	£1.	17. 6
1 Doddridge.. Sermons to young persons	2.	10
1 Baxter.. Saints Rest	5.	8
1 Doddridge on Regeneration	6	—
1 Mason on Self knowledge	4.	6
1 Edwards on the Affections	, 6.	6
1 —— Sermons	, 6	—
1 Hervey.. miditations	5.	6
1 Cooks Voyages 2 Vols	16.	6
1 Hutchinsons Massachusetts 2 Vols	1.	1 —
1 Ramsay.. history of the War 2 Vols	1.	1 —
1 Littletons history of England 2 Vols	10.	6
1 Morse Geography	4.	9
1 Milton.. paradise lost	5.	3
1 Youngs.. Night Thoughts	. 5	—
1 Thomsons Travels to the holy land 2 Vols	11.	6
1 Life of Baron Trenck	6.	6
1 Montagues Travels	4	—
1 Death of Abel	2.	6
1 pamela, Grandison & Clarissa abridg'd	4.	6
1 Vicar of Wakefield	3	—
1 Thomsons Seasons	2	—
	£9. 12. 6	
Discount 10 pr Cent	19.	3
	8. 13. 3	

Recd payment in full

In 1929, original bills of sale for the first books were found in the Main Street home of library committeeman Thomas Painter.

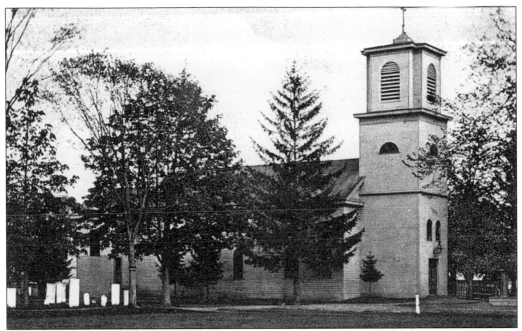

A second church that originally stood on West Haven Green is Christ Episcopal Church, founded in 1723. The first building was located perpendicular to the rear of the Congregational church building. Both churches shared the central burial grounds until Church Street was constructed in 1857, dividing the properties.

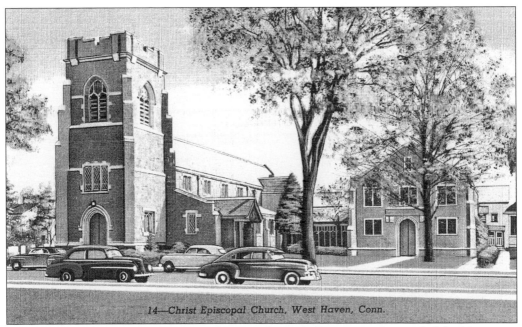

14—Christ Episcopal Church, West Haven, Conn.

A new Christ Episcopal Church, with a handsome bell tower and extended building, was constructed of stone in 1906. Timbers from the original wooden structure were used to build St. Martin-in-the-Field, a summer chapel on Washington Avenue and Park Street.

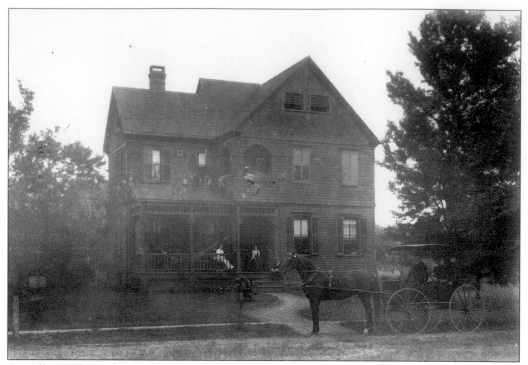

Carroll A. Shepard, seen in his buggy, visits the Christ Church rectory on Center Street around 1890.

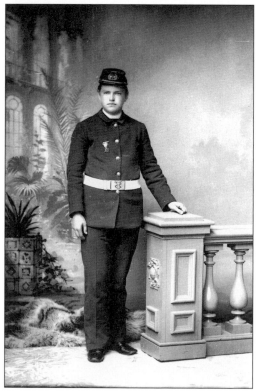

Carroll Shepard poses for his portrait around 1890.

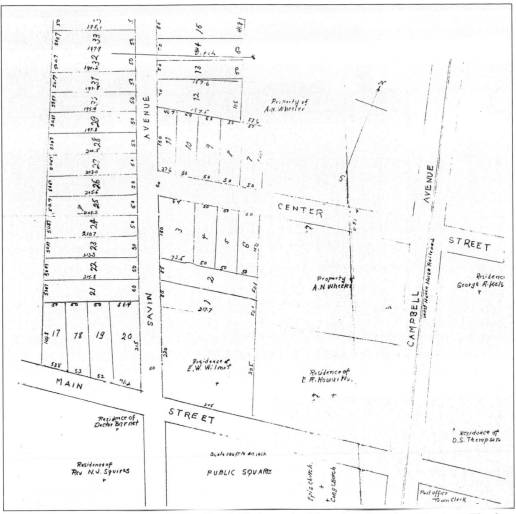

In 1888, landowner E. W. Wilmot offered 35 choice building lots for sale at auction. The lots were located one block west of town hall. Incentives included the cool breezes and quiet of an affordable country home and the accessibility of the new trolley line a block away. Wilmot lived on the northwest corner of Main Street and Campbell Avenue in a home that once belonged to Hannah Kimberly, organizer of the American Missionary Society.

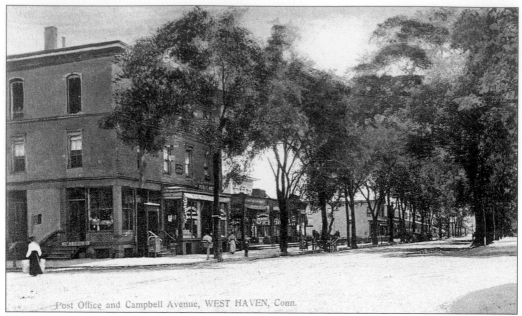

Post Office and Campbell Avenue, WEST HAVEN, Conn.

The 19th century was one of strong economic growth. Gracious homes of prominent citizens, businesses, and government offices surrounded the West Haven Green on all sides. The Thompson Building, on the northeast corner of Main Street and Campbell Avenue, housed the town clerk's office, post office, grocery, and coal and wood order shop. The Masonic Order met on the third floor of that building, which is known as the Feinson or Altschuler Building today.

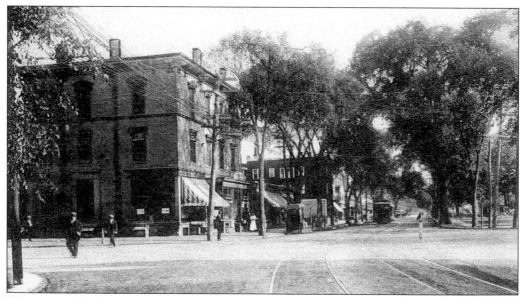

West Haven had developed electric lines for trolleys before New Haven did. The first electric trolleys carried guests to and from the center of the city to the shore and back on June 13, 1892.

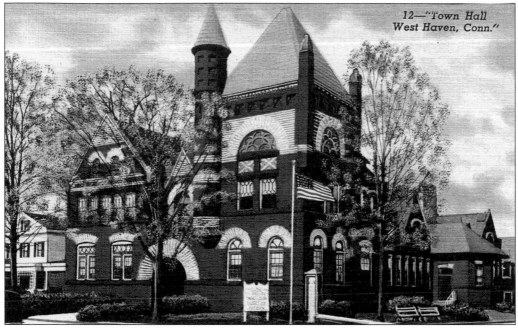

The rapid expansion of the Borough of West Haven warranted the construction of a town hall. In 1893, offices and an assembly room were built at the northwest corner of Main Street and Campbell Avenue. In 1932, the assembly room was converted to additional offices.

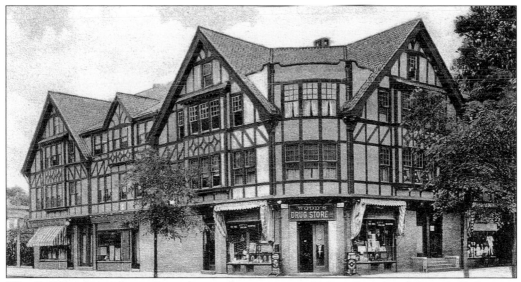

Wood's Drug Store, located on the northeast corner of Main Street and Campbell Avenue, was a three-story English Tudor–style building. Upper stories contained beautifully appointed residential quarters. Tradition holds, and today, the building houses Silver's Pharmacy, managed by a third-generation of the family with that name.

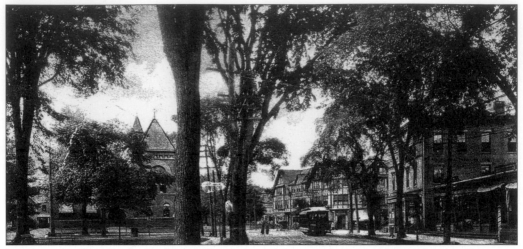

The view looking north on Campbell Avenue at the intersection of Main Street offers some perspective of the main intersection of the town in the late 19th century.

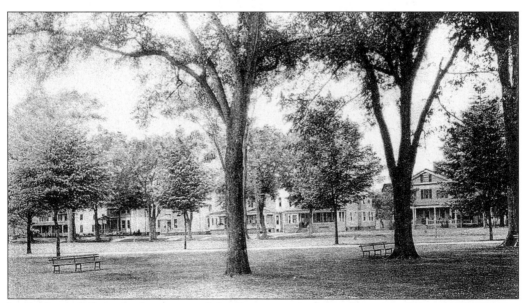

Looking north from the front steps of the Congregational church, one could see the fine homes located on Main Street adjacent to town hall.

Two

LOCAL BUSINESSES

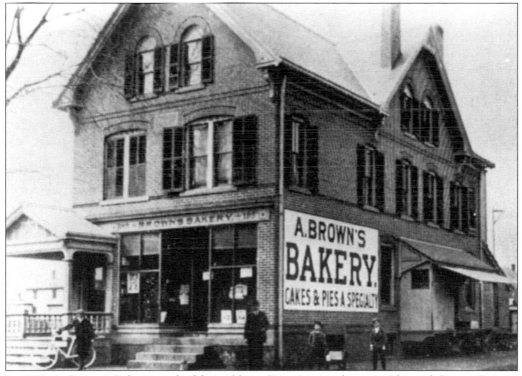

In 1894, A. Brown's Bakery was highly visible on First Avenue, between Elm and Center Streets. The shadow of this wall advertisement is still visible today.

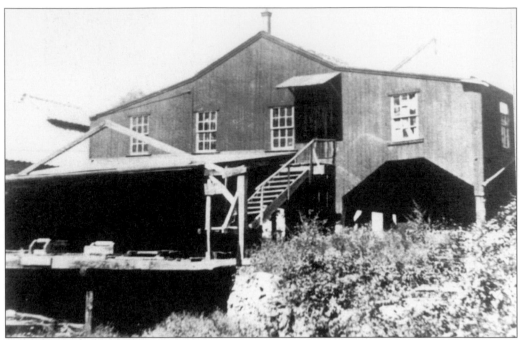

West Haven was heavily forested, and trees large enough for king's boards were readily available. Logs were cut in a two-man saw pit at the old red sawmill on Saw Mill Road.

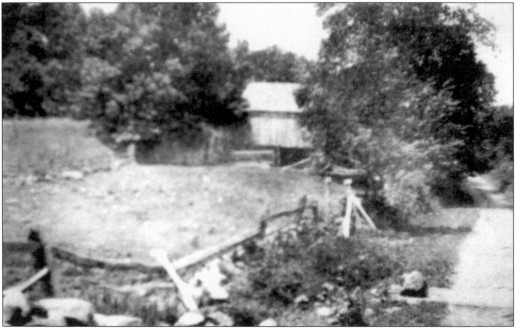

A sorghum mill, operated on the old Hubbard farm from 1862 to 1883, supplied the needs of West Haven, Milford, and Orange families. The cornlike plant was used for fodder and fuel, and during the Civil War, a molasses-like sugar substitute was made from the syrup of the plant.

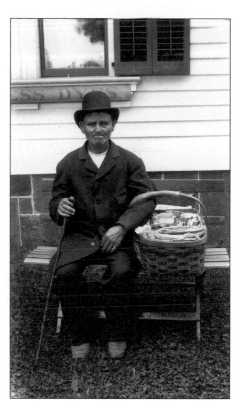

Not all business was conducted in stores. Door-to-door peddlers William O'Brian and Frances Ward were familiar faces. He sold dry goods and sundries, and she sold needles, thimbles, pins, lace, and other small sewing items.

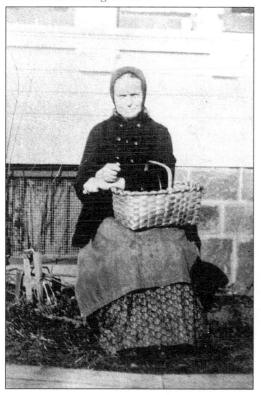

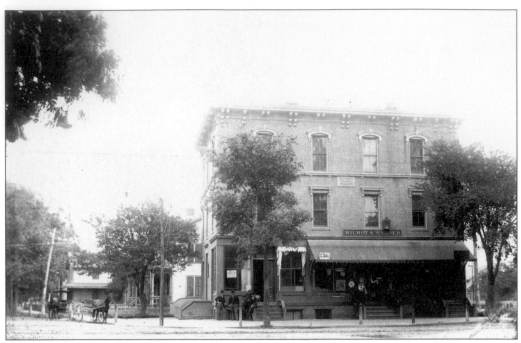

One could conveniently order coal or wood at Wilmot and Warner, a well-established grocer in the old Thompson Building.

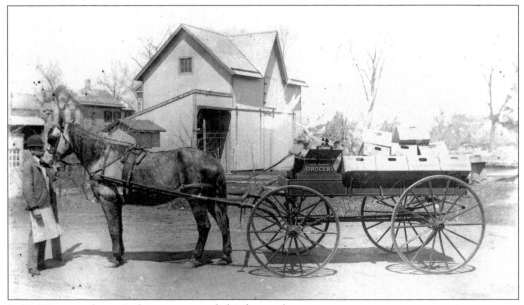

L. H. Warner, always in his apron, used this horse-drawn wagon to transport groceries.

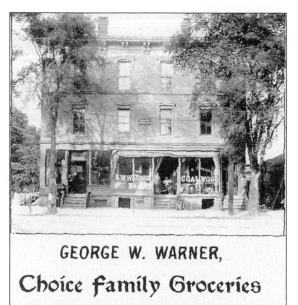

GEORGE W. WARNER,

Choice Family Groceries

FLOUR, FEED, FRUIT, ETC.

195 CAMPBELL AVENUE,
(P. O. BUILDING.)

Receive orders for
The D. T. Welch Co. Coal and Wood.   **WEST HAVEN, CONN.**

In 1900, George W. Warner Groceries and D. T. Welch Company, Coal and Wood advertised their services.

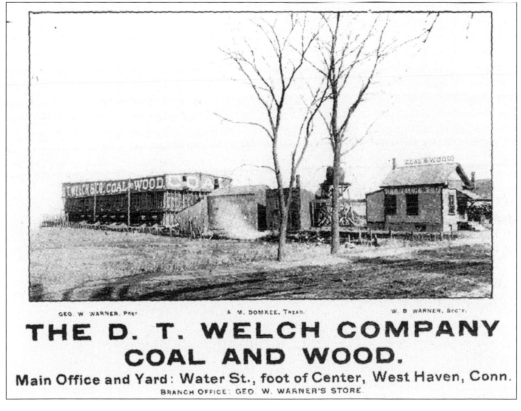

GEO. W. WARNER, Pres.   A. M. DOMKEE, Treas.   W. B. WARNER, Sec'y.

THE D. T. WELCH COMPANY
COAL AND WOOD.

Main Office and Yard: Water St., foot of Center, West Haven, Conn.
BRANCH OFFICE: GEO. W. WARNER'S STORE.

23

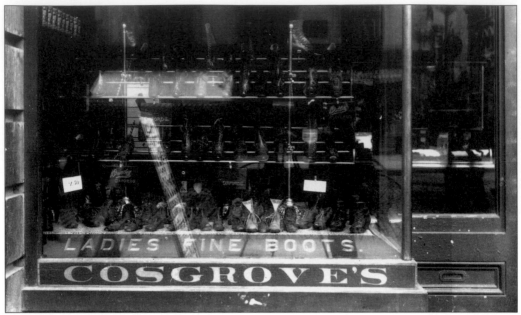

Cosgrove's Bootery carried a full line of ready-made, fashionable shoes and boots in all sizes, which could be purchased for $1.50 a pair.

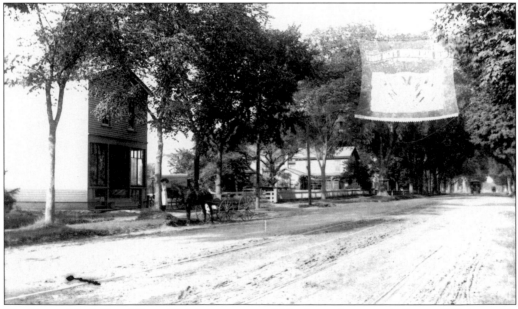

The Young Men's Republican Club banner waves high above the street in front of Wadsworth's Tin Shop.

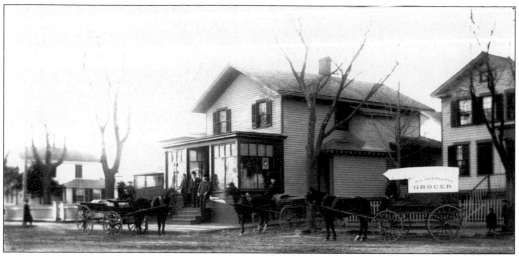

As the town's population rapidly increased, so did the number of grocers. Horse-drawn wagons and delivery carts meant fresh produce reached tables quickly from the Nettleton Grocery on Elm Street.

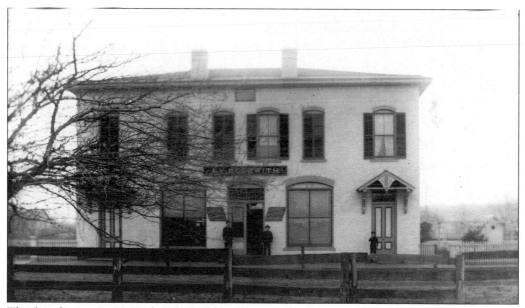

The handsome A. V. Beckwith Building housed the Ennever Grocery. In early 1800, West Haven had two main streets and 40 houses. By 1900, the population had expanded appreciably and businesses and services flourished.

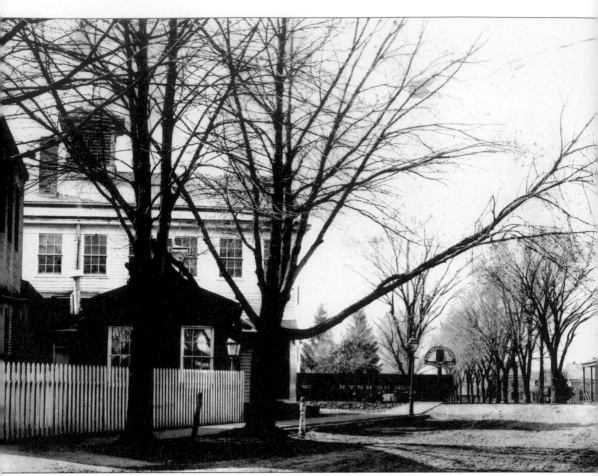

The West Haven Buckle Company, on Washington Avenue, was incorporated in 1853. Two names are synonymous with the success of the business: Sheldon S. Hartshorn, who patented the first hinged buckle made in America, and entrepreneur George Kelsey. The product line included brass or steel metal specialties such as hooks, strap and belt buckles, slide bars, links and suspender rings, button loops, and handles in many sizes and styles. Civil War injuries increased the demand for clamps, limb snaps, fasteners and links, and brass or surgical hooks, buckles, slide bars, links and suspender rings, and truss rings for use with prostheses.

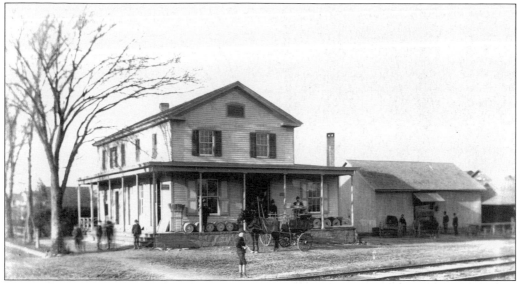

The Sherwood Bishop Grocery was located on the street on the opposite side of the railroad tracks, diagonally across from the West Haven Buckle Company on Washington Avenue. Sherwood Bishop was the father of Yale Bishop and father-in-law of Frank Wilcox, both Savin Rock restaurant owners.

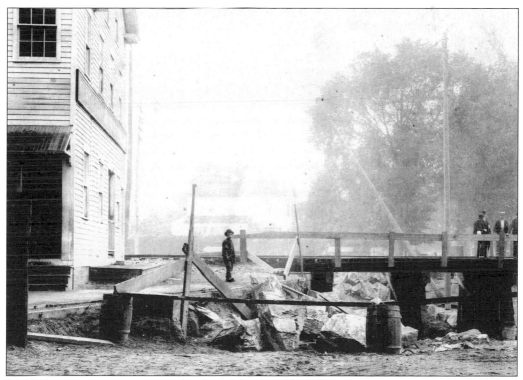

In 1895, concern over increased rail and local traffic led to the construction of a vehicular underpass in front of the West Haven Buckle Company at the intersection of Wood Street and Washington Avenue.

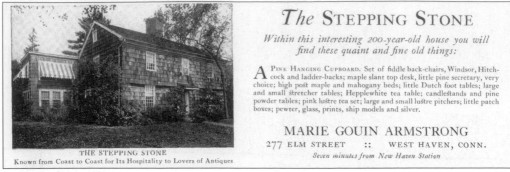

Marie Gouin Armstrong advertised her Elm Street Stepping Stone antiques shop in the November 1924 issue of *Antiques*, a monthly publication.

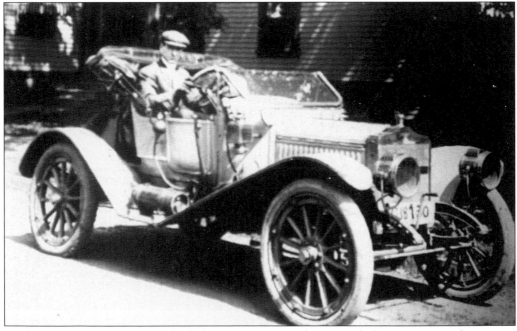

Arthur Gouin was the envy of all the young men, as he sported about town in a luxury car produced by flying ace Eddie Rickenbacker.

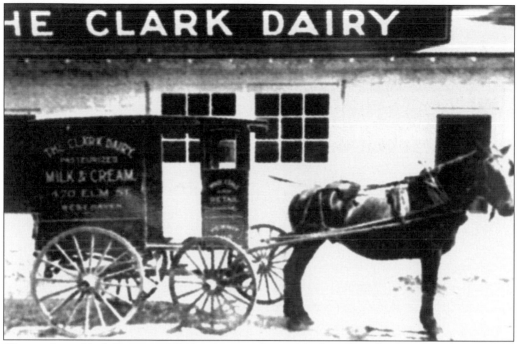

Wagons from Clark Dairy, at 470 Elm Street, delivered fresh milk and cream daily. When John T. Clark discovered he could not use all of the milk his cows supplied, he decided to sell the oversupply to his neighbors. His brother and two sons went into the business, which grew to 12 horses and wagons and then to several trucks covering all area towns.

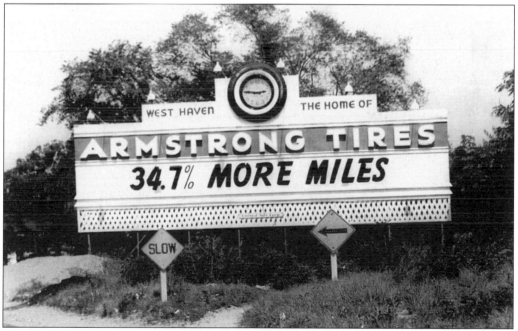

A roadside billboard advertises Armstrong Tires in 1939. Founded in 1912, the company moved to West Haven in 1922. James A. Walsh, president, was credited with the redesign of tires. The company was a major producer of tires and rubber rafts during World War II.

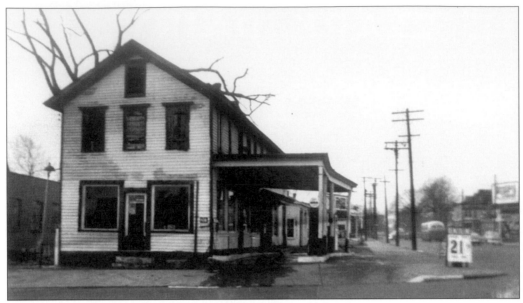

The Benzoline gas station stood on the corner of Elm and Water Streets.

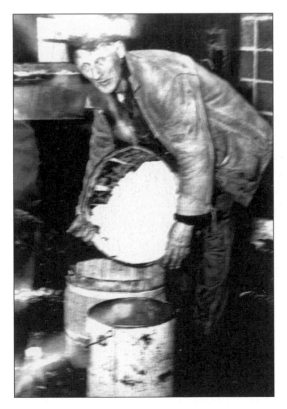

Before refrigerators, there were iceboxes. Iceman Bill Hearns delivered blocks of ice to local homes. The size of the block was determined by a sign that residents placed in a window.

Three

FAMILIES AT HOME

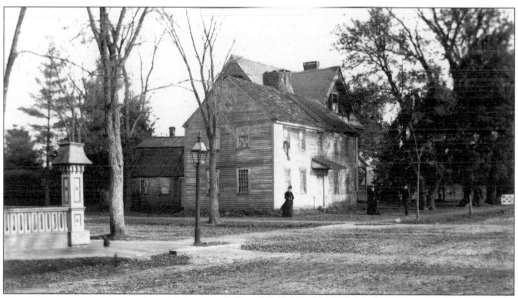

The Hine family's first home on Main Street was typical of the well-constructed, early two-over-two homesteads built in West Haven. This elegant house also had a large hearth room, or great room, in the rear.

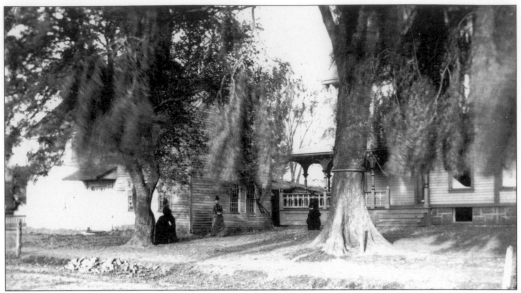

The Hines had a later Victorian Gothic home, built around 1868, which featured a large porch with exquisite detail.

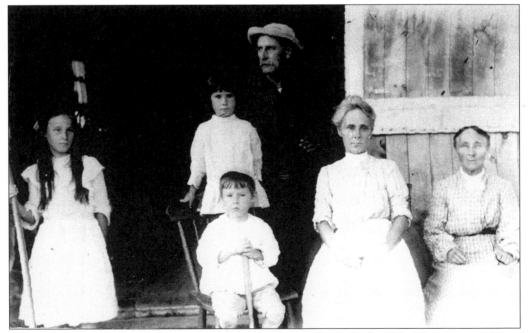

The Parkers lived on First Avenue. Daughter Dot Parker (with the long dark hair) married into the Hine family.

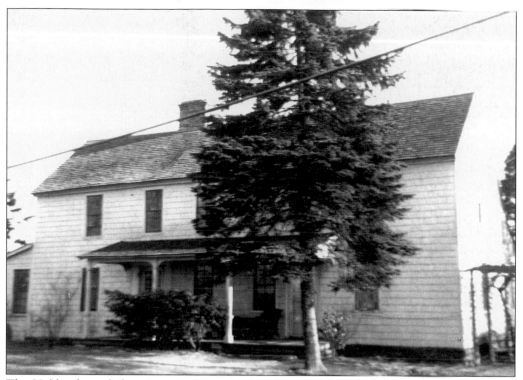

The Hubbards settled on Jones Hill Road. Their beautiful large farmhouse was a stop on the Underground Railroad. Slaves were hidden in a secret space in the upper story.

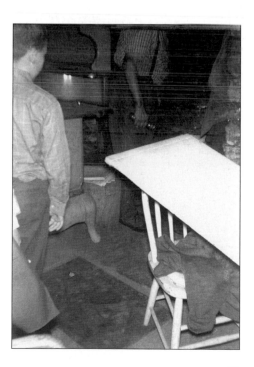

A legless slave table, which folded out of the wall in the large Hubbard kitchen, was used when additional meals were served.

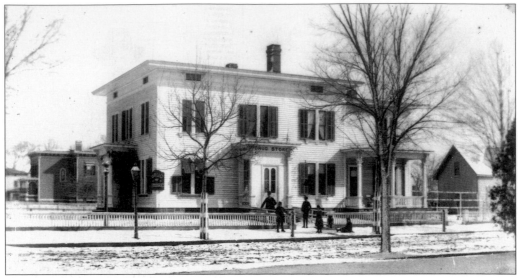

Dr. Durrell Shepard's fine residence and pharmacy, on the corner of Washington Avenue and Elm Street, is now recognized as the Keenan Funeral Home.

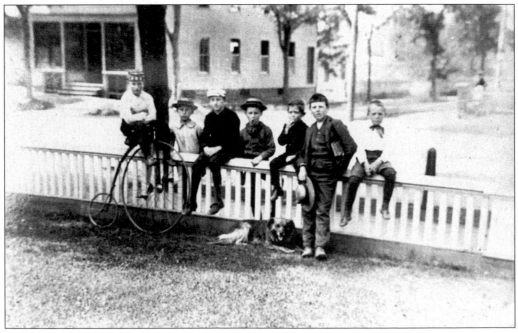

Young lads preferred fence sitting while visiting with Charles Shepard (far left).

A bearded Dr. Durrell Shepard poses in his Civil War hat and medals around 1890.

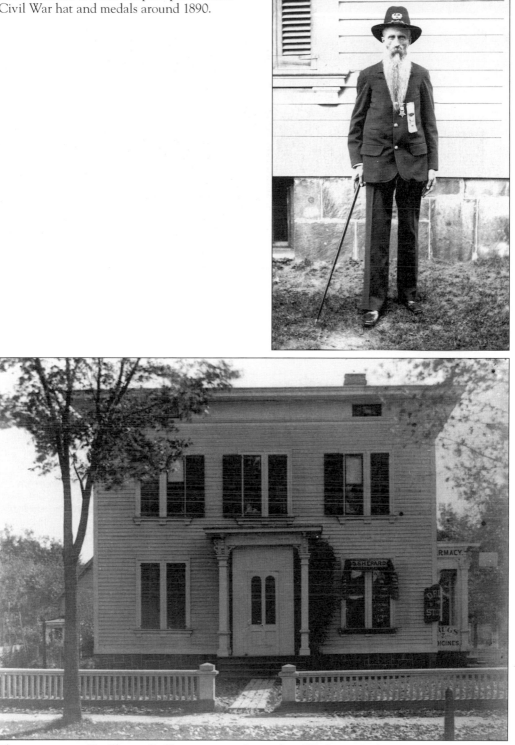

The entrance to Dr. Shepard's Pharmacy was located on Washington Avenue.

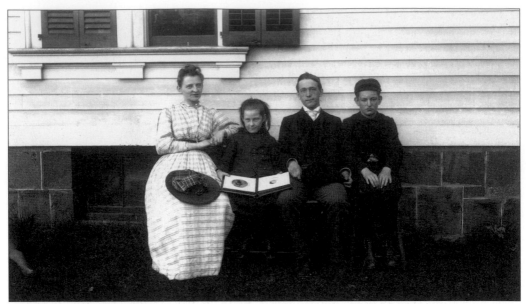

George, Gussie, Lillie, and Charles Shepard pose with a family photograph album.

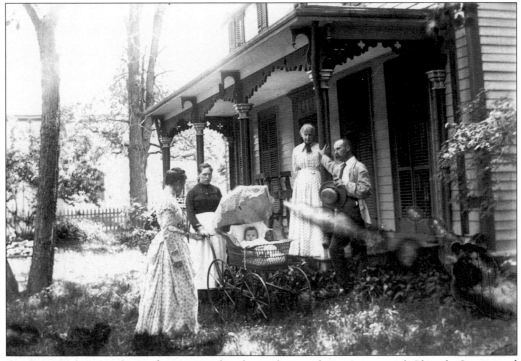

Dr. Barnet, his family, and a nanny lived on the southeast corner of Church Street and Savin Avenue.

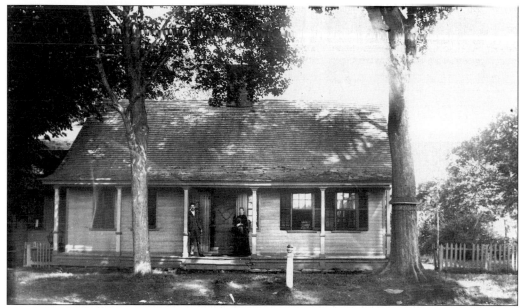

Mrs. James Tolles stands on the porch of the old Tolles home, on Elm Street near Deacon's Lane (now Union Street).

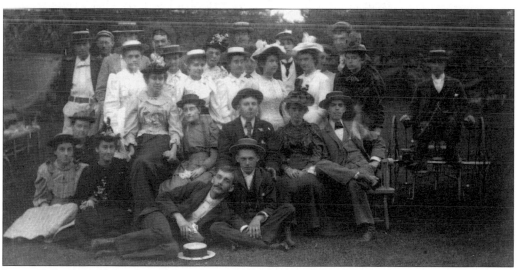

James Tolles hosted family and friends on the Fourth of July 1892.

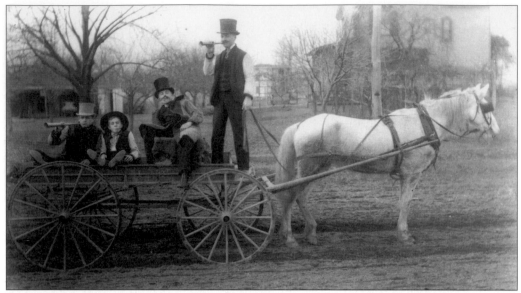

The Messiers Tuttle, McLellan, Tolles, and Cosgrove celebrate with a horn party.

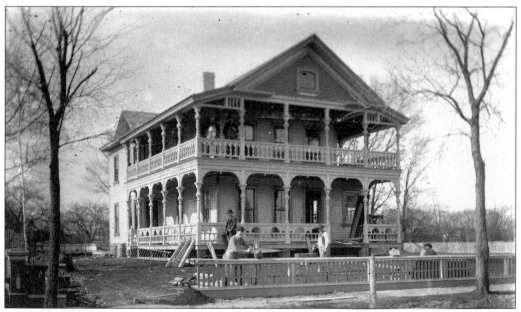

The Israel Kelsey house is under construction in 1890 on the site of the present-day Knight of Columbus Building.

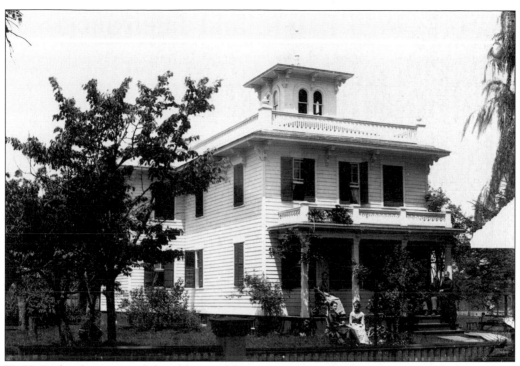

H. H. Richards, owner of the oldest and longest operating lumber company and shipyard on Water Street, lived on Main Street near the corner of Second Avenue.

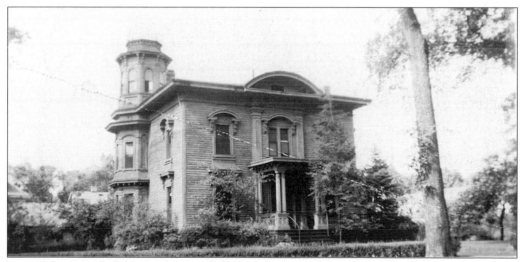

Capt. John Marshall Richards owned Hedgehurst, which was located at the corner of Main Street and Second Avenue.

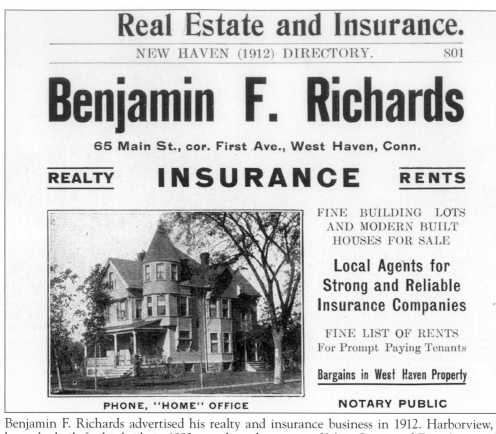

Real Estate and Insurance.

Benjamin F. Richards

65 Main St., cor. First Ave., West Haven, Conn.

REALTY   **INSURANCE**   **RENTS**

FINE BUILDING LOTS
AND MODERN BUILT
HOUSES FOR SALE

**Local Agents for
Strong and Reliable
Insurance Companies**

FINE LIST OF RENTS
For Prompt Paying Tenants

Bargains in West Haven Property

PHONE, "HOME" OFFICE   **NOTARY PUBLIC**

Benjamin F. Richards advertised his realty and insurance business in 1912. Harborview, the home he built for his bride in 1892, stands at the corner of Main Street and First Avenue. The cabinetry in his former office was designed as modular units and was made of the finest woods, similar to those on the sailing ships his family company produced.

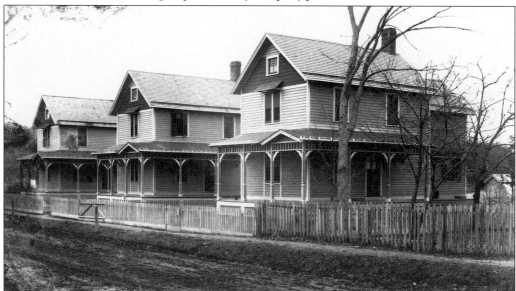

The Richards family owned several summer cottages on Richards Street.

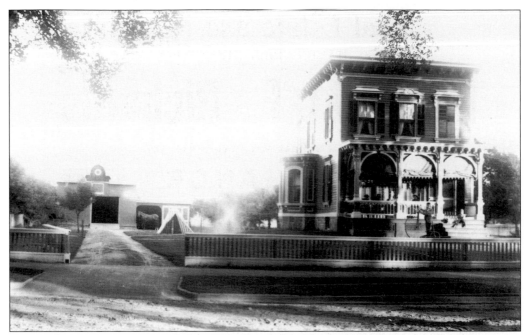

C. E. Thompson, treasurer of the West Haven Buckle Company, entertains guests on his large sun-shaded porch. The younger Mr. Thompson shows off his fashionable bicycle, which he enjoyed riding around town. The family horse stands by the carriage house, behind the children's playground.

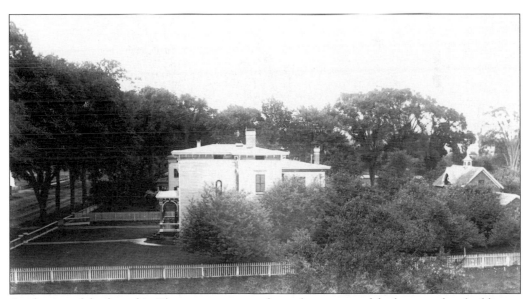

A side view of the fenced-in Thompson property shows the expanse of the lawns and outbuildings.

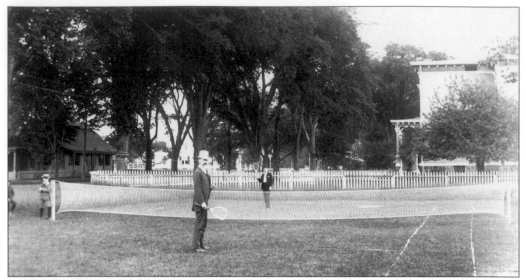

Appropriately attired ladies and gentlemen enjoy a game of tennis on the Thompson lawn adjacent to the house.

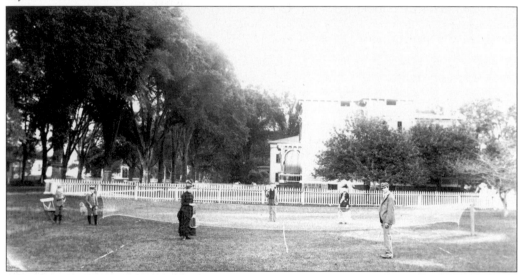

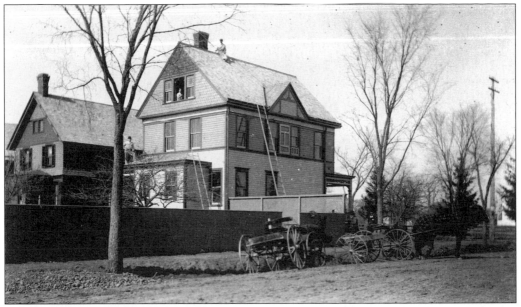

The Thompsons, like many affluent West Haven families, owned town houses and cottages where they spent the summer season. The materials needed for the construction of the Thompson cottage were brought by horse and wagon around 1891.

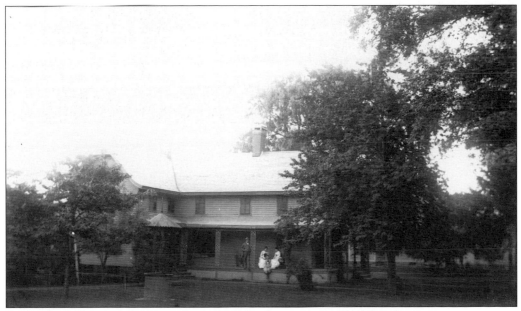

D. S. Thompson poses with members of his family on the porch of their home.

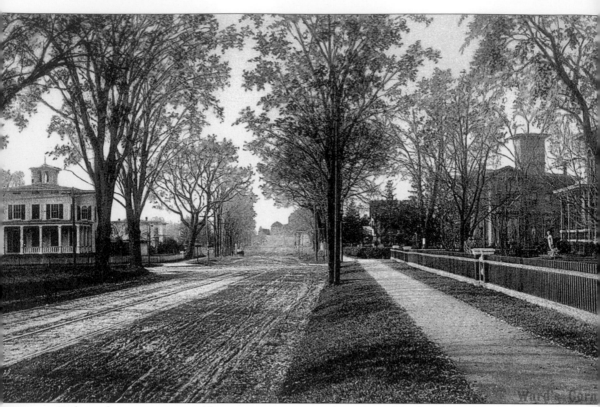

Perhaps the most recognizable intersection in a residential neighborhood was Wards Corner, the junction of Campbell Avenue and Elm Street. Several Ward family members owned fine homes at and around each corner, as may be seen in this view looking westward on Elm Street. The building at the far left was later known as the Phelps Mansion, where Marjorie Phelps had her popular nursery school.

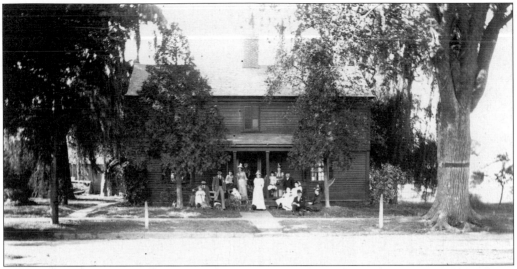

The Ward home on Elm Street was originally owned by Rebecca Clark, the daughter of one of the first settlers of West Farms. It would not have been unusual to see a large gathering at the home, as the Ward family was large, successful, and respected. Jacob Ward was the father of Minott, Fred, George, William Wallace, Israel, and Louisa Ward.

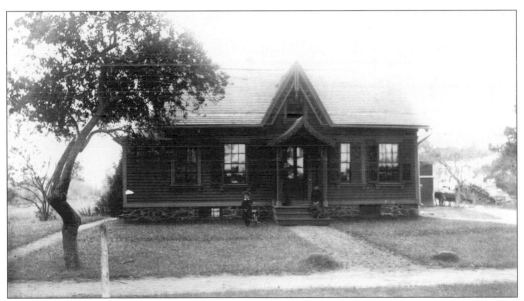

The old Ward cottage, located at the corner of Campbell Avenue and Ashburton Place, belonged to Capt. Jacob Ward.

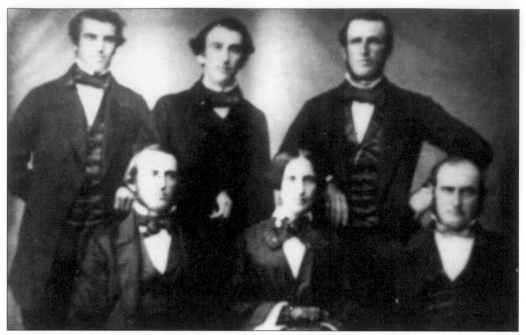

Several of the Ward brothers and their father were seamen, both in international trade and in the military service. Louisa Ward married Adrienne C. Heitmann and remained in the Elm Street house. The couple's daughter Henrietta was the headmistress of Miss Heitmann's School for Dames.

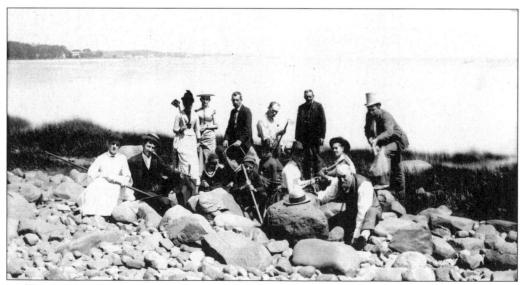

Wallace W. Ward and guests dig for clams at Oyster River Bay, near his family cottage.

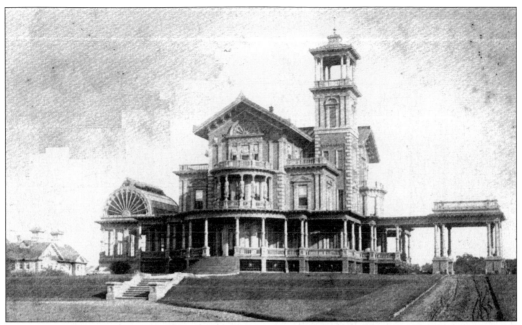

The Waddingham Mansion was considered the showplace of its day in all of New England. Wilson W. Waddingham owned the Emma (gold) Mine in the Black Hills and large cattle ranches in New Mexico. He spared no expense on the home, paying attention to every detail from the unique woods and custom-designed stained glass windows, tall porticos, and exquisite solarium, to the alfresco paintings in the billiards room. His guests were lavishly entertained in a luxurious environment. The property was bounded by First Avenue, Elm Street, Third Avenue, and Wood Street. After the vacant house burned to the ground on October 16, 1903, the bricks were used to build row houses on Third Avenue. The carriage house still stands near the end of Third Avenue.

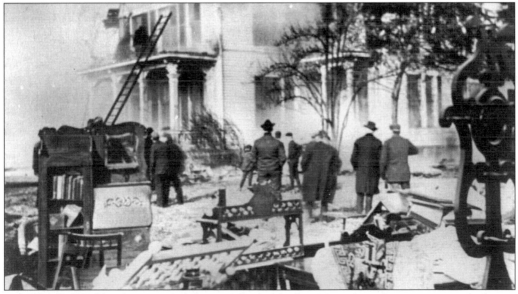

In 1906, the Waddingham caretaker's cottage caught fire. Many furnishings were emptied onto the front lawn, including a black walnut hat stand and a golden oak desk.

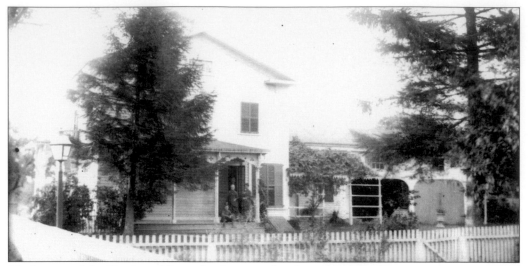

The houses of the Tuttle and Price families were familiar edifices in the community.

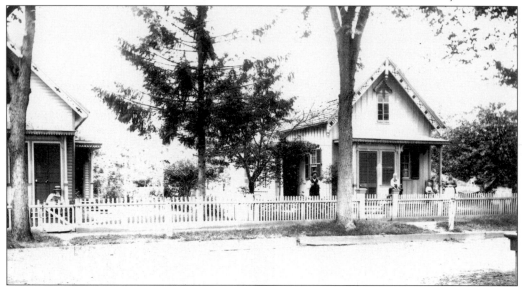

Four

EVENTS AND PERSONALITIES

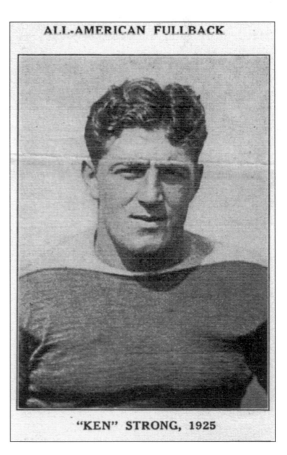

ALL-AMERICAN FULLBACK

"KEN" STRONG, 1925

In 1928, West Haven High School honored a favorite son, All-American football star Ken Strong (class of 1924). He was met at the Washington Avenue train station by a large welcoming crowd and was escorted to West Haven High by the school band. A pubic reception and a program were held in his honor. Some years later, the city dedicated Ken Strong Stadium.

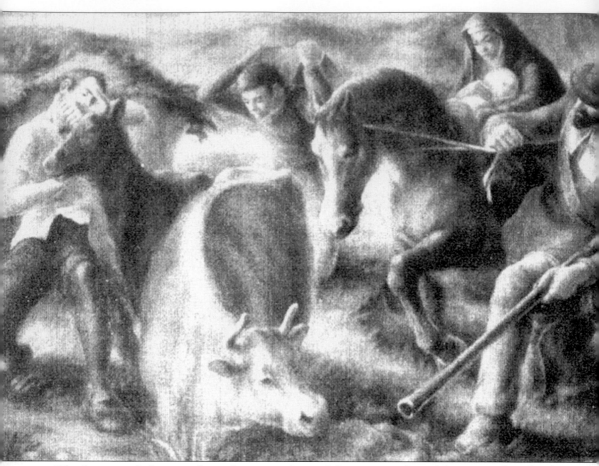

The first recorded event of significance in the city's history was that of the move of six families to the promising farming and grazing land known as West Farms. A stunning re-creation of the

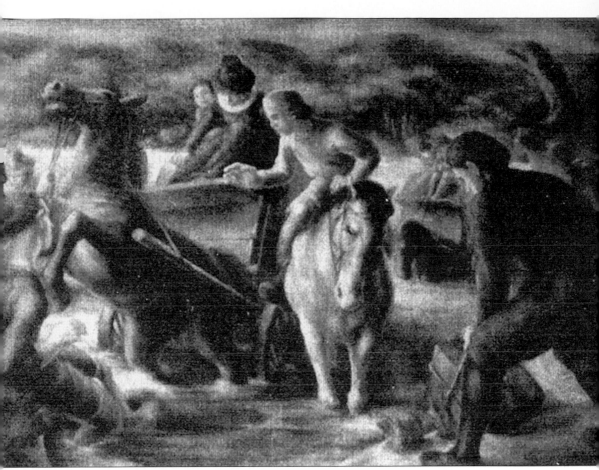

event, *Crossing the West River – 1648,* by artist Elizabeth Shannon Phelps, can be seen in the post office on Campbell Avenue, where the work was installed in 1937 as a federal arts project.

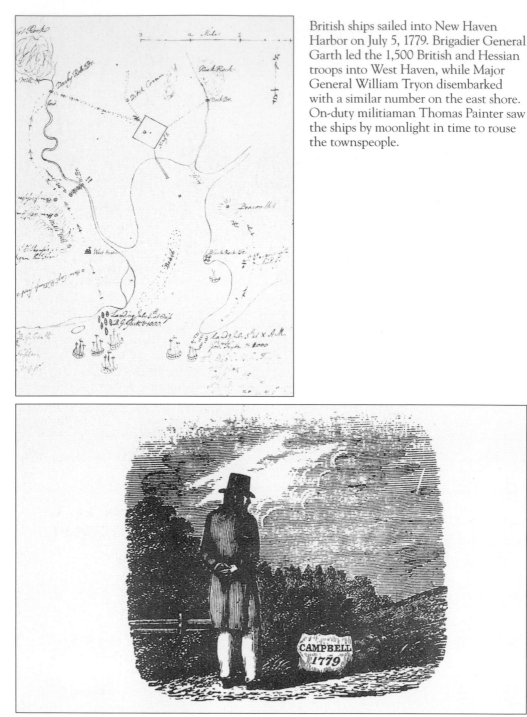

British ships sailed into New Haven Harbor on July 5, 1779. Brigadier General Garth led the 1,500 British and Hessian troops into West Haven, while Major General William Tryon disembarked with a similar number on the east shore. On-duty militiaman Thomas Painter saw the ships by moonlight in time to rouse the townspeople.

The Reverend Noah Williston is buried in the central burial grounds of the Congregational church on West Haven Green, along with Thomas Painter and other patriots of the Revolutionary War. Williston was captured by Hessian soldiers as he attempted to hide town records, which had been kept in the meetinghouse. Adj. William Campbell of the British forces mercifully ordered his release, a deed which Williston celebrated each year until his death.

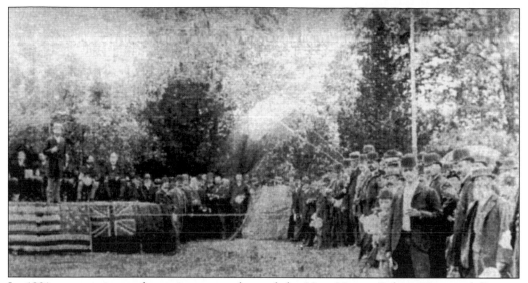

In 1891, a committee of prominent members of the New Haven Colony Historical Society dedicated a large monument at the grave site of Adj. William Campbell to replace the original smaller marker located nearer to the street. Preparation for the well-attended event included research, fund-raising, and extensive correspondence with Queen Victoria. When Campbell was mortally wounded near Milford Hill (Allingtown), local landowners Mary Alling and John Prudden donated small strips of land for his burial in respect for his kind deed earlier in the day. The parklike site was refurbished in 1991 through a grant from the City of West Haven.

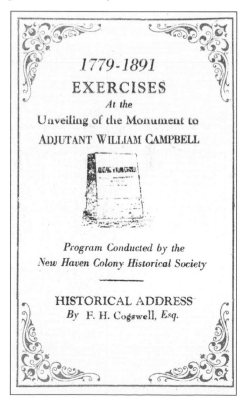

A Program of the Day includes the major speech and events of the day.

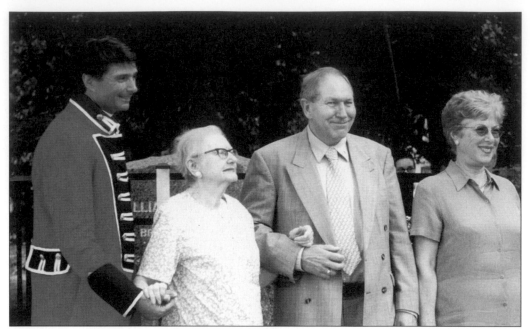

From left to right, Mayor H. Richard Borer and West Haven Historical Society president Margaret Mayer join British Vice-Counsel and Mrs. Geoff Plante at the rededication ceremony of the William Campbell grave site in August 1991.

Schedule of Activities

10 a.m.	*General Muster, all Regional Marching Units, Fife and Drum Corps, and British Representatives at Old Grove Park, Palace and Oak Streets*
11 a.m.	*Arrival at Center Green, Fall into Formation*
11:30 a.m.	*Reenactment of Incident with the Rev. Williston* *Wreath Laying on the Green by British Delegation* *Regiments Stroll, Perform on Green*
1 p.m.	*Regiments Fall In, March to Grave Site Monument of Adjutant William Campbell of the Brigade of British Guards*
1:45 p.m.	*Regiments Form Honor Guard for Dignitaries on Pruden Street*
2 p.m.	*Grave Site Rededication Ceremony by British and American Dignitaries*

The day began with a parade retracing the route of the British troops, with several New England reenactment groups led by 2nd Company Governor's Foot Guard and 1st Company Horse Guard. The *Williston Incident* was reenacted on the West Haven Green, and then the entire company marched to the grave site and finally to a dignitaries' reception hosted by Pres. Lawrence DeNardis of the University of New Haven.

In 1853, at age 15, Charles Sherwood Stratton left his West Haven family home to join P. T. Barnum's circus, and forever after was known as Tom Thumb. It is believed that this 1863 wedding picture of Tom and his bride, Lavinia Warren, was taken at his family home at 768 Campbell Avenue. Other wedding group photographs seem to confirm this setting. According to relatives, he was four years old when his mother moved the family from a house she had built on Campbell Avenue at Highland Street to No. 768 Campbell. He maintained contact with his family and friends in West Haven until his death in Massachusetts in 1883.

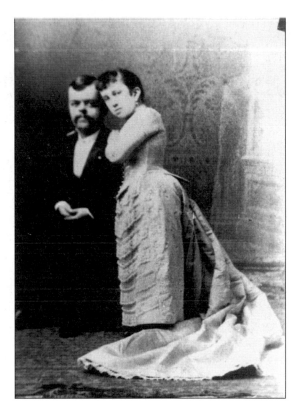

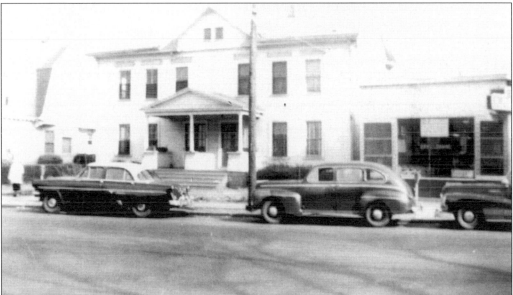

The famous Malley murder case, in which young Edward Malley of the department store family was accused of drowning a young lady in Long Island Sound, was tried in the West Haven Town Court. The defendant was represented by the grandfather of Harriet C. North, city historian. The building was moved from the lot where Silver's Pharmacy now stands to the corner of Curtis Place and Campbell Avenue.

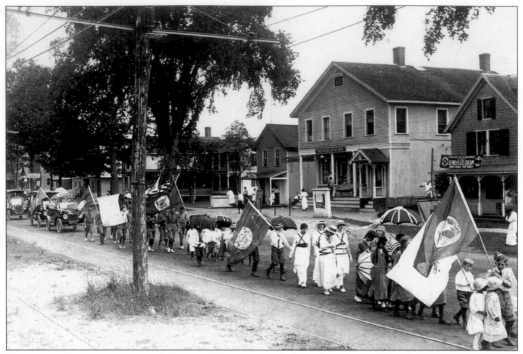

Townspeople were always ready for a celebration, including these young people parading with flags and banners past the People's Store and Semon's Ice Cream Parlor one summer around 1890.

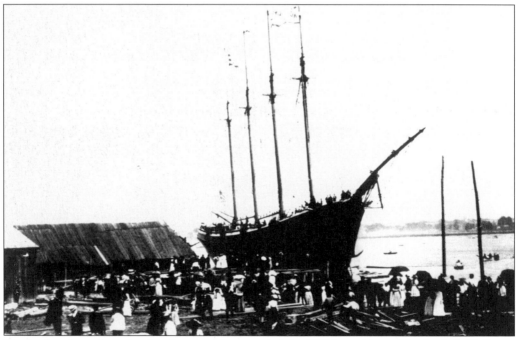

Picnics, bands, and an air of excitement accompanied the 1891 launching of the *Lucinda K. Sutton* at the Gesner & Mar Shipyard, on Water Street. The *Sutton*, the last of the commercial sailing vessels built by West Haven shipyards, was launched at low tide and became mired in mud.

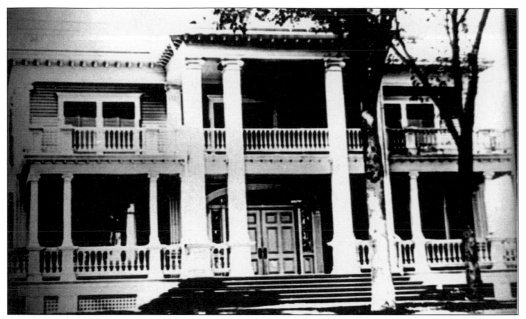

Connecticut's governor, lieutenant governor, and committee decided to preserve the Connecticut House of the Columbia Exhibition of 1893. Piece by piece, the house was moved to the Colonial Park section of Ocean Avenue and rebuilt on property donated by Wilson Waddingham. The Red Cross used the building during World War I until fire from a caretaker's burning leaves destroyed the house in 1918.

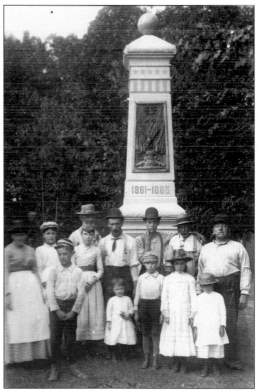

Families honor fallen heroes with a visit to the Soldiers and Sailors Monument in Oak Grove Cemetery around July 1890.

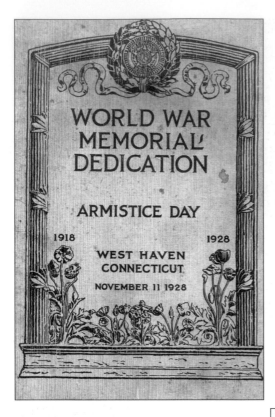

On November 11, 1928, a full 10 years to the day of the signing of the armistice, the Hughson Post No. 71, American Legion dedicated a memorial to those who fought and died in the war to end all wars. The daylong program included a parade of military, fraternal, and civilian organizations, dedication services, patriotic songs, roll call, taps, and a dinner.

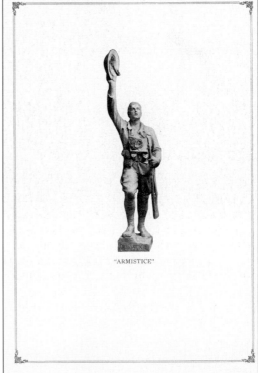

"ARMISTICE"

Armistice, the granite and bronze World War I monument that stands on the green facing Main Street, replaced an honor roll that listed the names of all military personnel of the war.

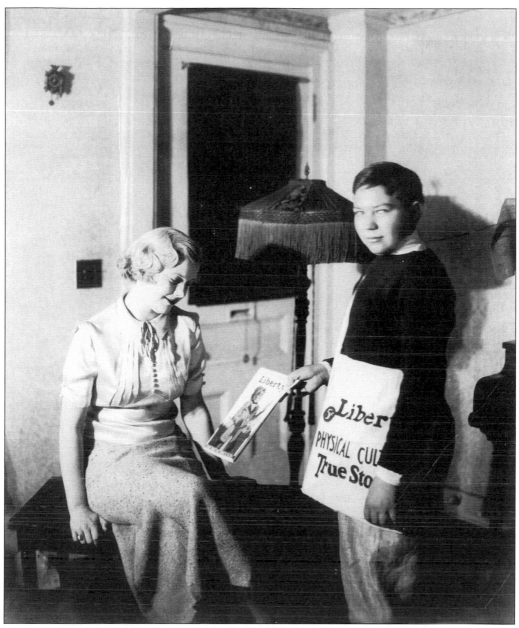

A young Fredrick Kaercher delivers *Liberty* magazine to Miss America, 1933, Marion Bergeron of West Haven, who actually won the title twice. After it was discovered that she was underage, she was allowed to enter the competition the next year, again winning the honor. West Haven can also boast of a Junior Miss America and a Miss Teen America.

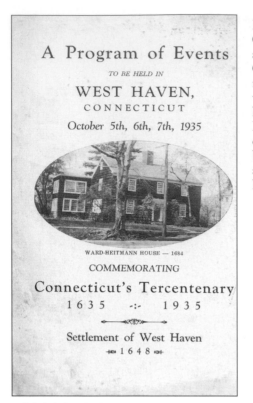

A Program of Events

TO BE HELD IN

WEST HAVEN,

CONNECTICUT

October 5th, 6th, 7th, 1935

WARD-HEITMANN HOUSE — 1684

COMMEMORATING

Connecticut's Tercentenary

1 6 3 5   -:-   1 9 3 5

Settlement of West Haven

1 6 4 8

In October 1935, three days were dedicated to the Connecticut tercentenary celebration. There was a parade, a ball, exhibits, visits to Adj. William Campbell's grave site, and bronze souvenir medals and plates. Guides, maps, and postcards were also available. A Saturday luncheon was held at Miss Hamilton's Tearoom in the Ward-Heitmann House. On Sunday, Congregational church worshipers were summoned to service by drummers in a "service of the old order;" the afternoon was filled with music, speeches, and a historical pageant at the high school.

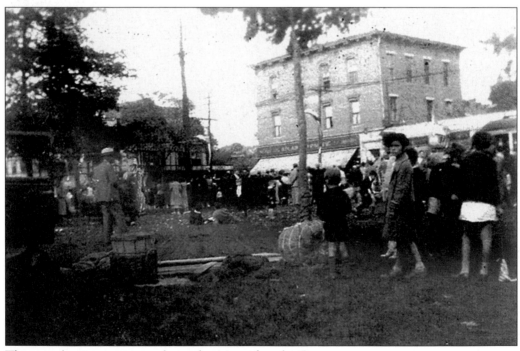

The tree planting ceremony drew a large crowd to the Green.

A man is dwarfed by the massive tree uprooted by the Hurricane of 1938, which slammed the West Haven shoreline with no advance warning. Power lines were downed, and streets were flooded, as seen here in front of Pfaff's Store on Elm Street.

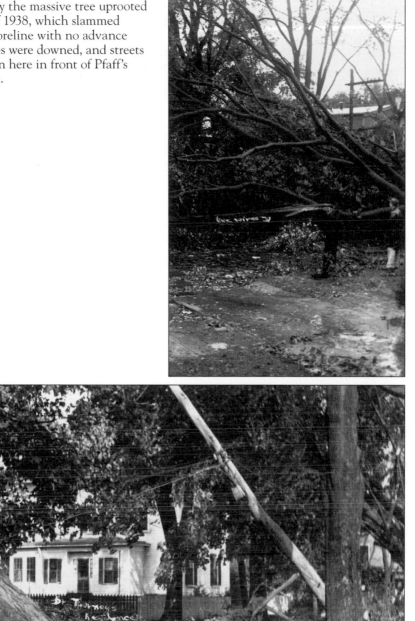

Sidewalks and streets rippled in the rear of Dr. Lawrence Tierney's house on Washington Avenue.

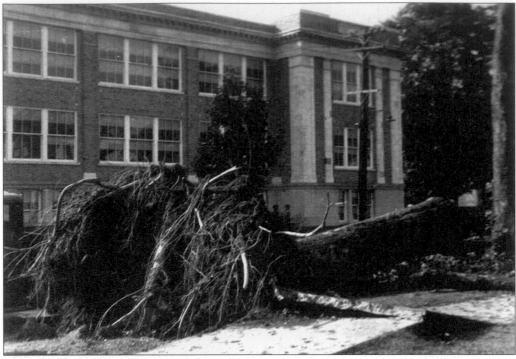

Frantic parents rushed to the schools as the storm built in intensity. Huge elm trees lifted sidewalks, such as the one in front of the high school.

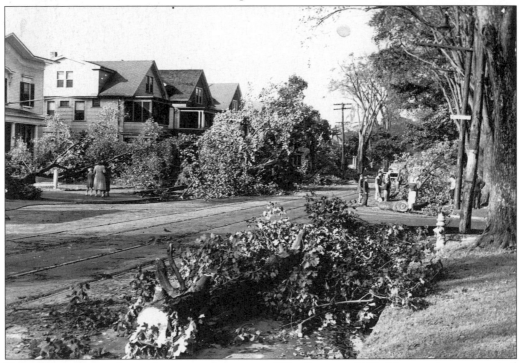

Folks survey the hurricane damage at the corner of Elm Street and Washington Avenue, typical of the entire region.

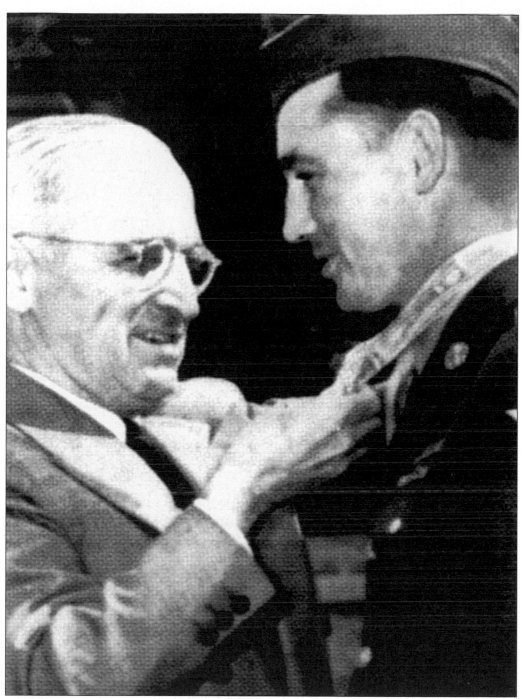

Pfc. William Soderman received the Medal of Honor from Pres. Harry Truman in 1945 for valor on the battlefield. Under cover of darkness and at point blank range, Soderman fired a bazooka into a German tank. From his foxhole, he provided cover for his withdrawing and reassembling company, hitting two more lead tanks before being wounded in the shoulder. When it was learned in 1995 that the U.S. Navy had named one of five sealift ships after the Medal of Honor winner, the city marked that event with a celebration and dedication ceremony at Bradley Point.

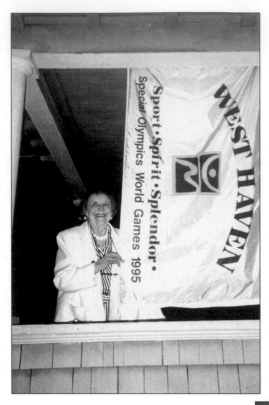

Harriet C. North, former city historian and society president, served as goodwill ambassador to the 1995 Special Olympics World Games in West Haven.

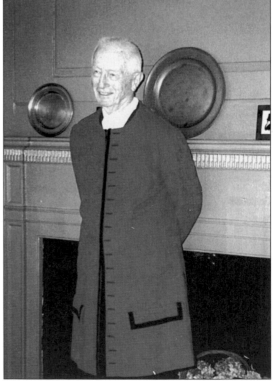

Bennett W. "Bill" Dorman, city historian, plays the role of a squire during a special event. Dorman, a noted authority on the Savin Rock Amusement Park, is a trustee and past president of the West Haven Historical Society.

Five

FAMILIAR SIGHTS

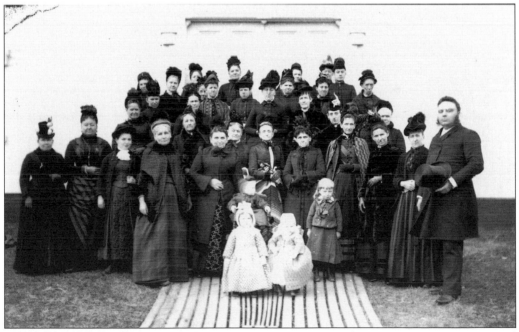

Somberly clad ladies of the original Methodist Episcopal Church, on Center Street at Second Avenue, pose with their minister around 1890.

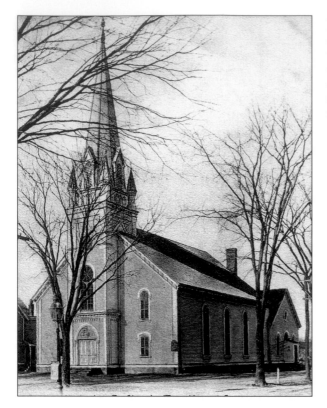

From 1868, Methodist Episcopal services were held every Sunday morning and every Thursday evening in Thompson's Hall. The congregation, with sufficient funds and 31 members, laid a cornerstone for a church on August 16, 1870.

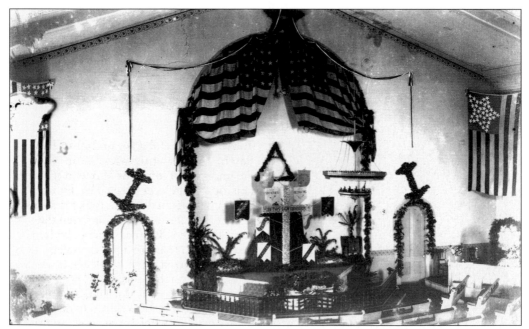

The interior of the original wooden Methodist church was decorated for a traditional holiday around 1891. By 1916, a new and larger stone church stood in the place of the original wooden building.

The cemeteries on the West Haven Green were once a single burial ground. In 1857, it was decided by mutual consent that a road should be created between the properties. The Williston and Stebbins family stones, bodies, and monuments were removed to the southwest corner of the Old Burial Grounds. Stones that date from about 1711 to the mid-1800s present a virtual tour of the history of West Haven, from founding families to Revolutionary War patriots and town leaders.

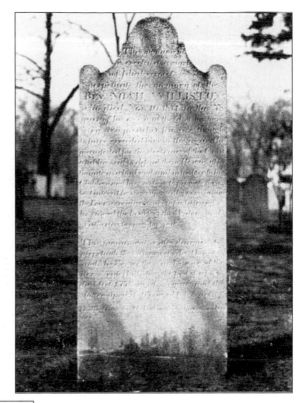

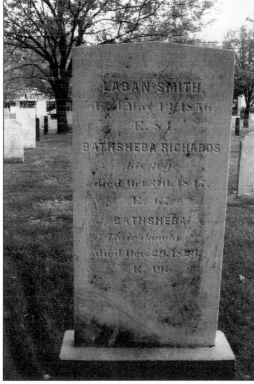

Today, the peaceful grave of Bathsheba Smith, who died at the age of 19 in 1823, lies under a spreading shade tree in the quiet Episcopal church cemetery. The day after the young woman died, her father returned to visit the cemetery and discovered the grave had been disturbed and her body was missing. He aroused the caretaker, and soon a crowd gathered. When it was determined that her corpse had been stolen by students of the Yale Medical School, the crowd marched to New Haven to demand her return. The scene turned ugly, and the Governor's Foot Guard was called. The body was returned to its proper burial site.

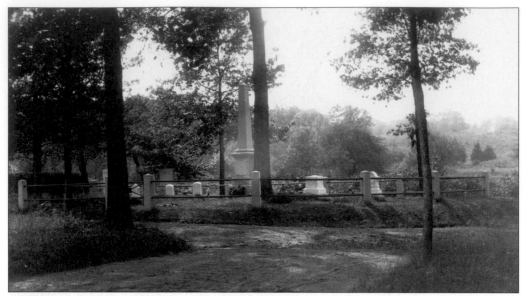

Oak Grove Cemetery, at the corner of Campbell Avenue and Spring Street, was developed when it was apparent that the cemeteries in the center of town were reaching capacity. The Tuttle family section is recognized by the tall marker on the grave of Cyrus Tuttle.

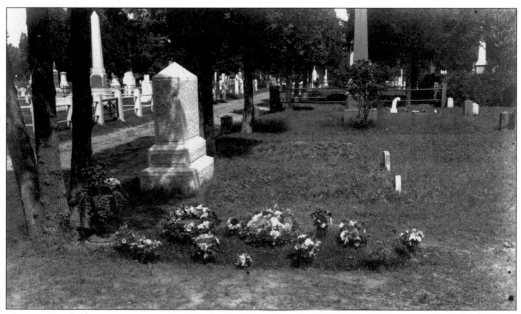

Flowers mark the new grave of a Martha L. Hartshorn in July 1891. The grounds of Oak Grove were spacious and well manicured.

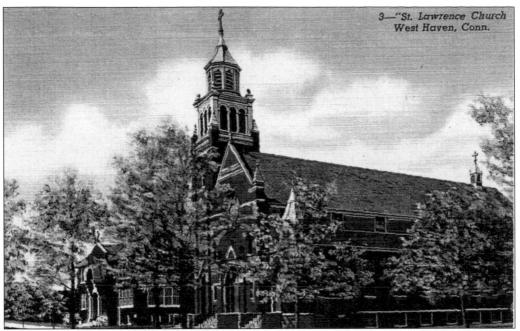

In April 1886, a mission church was established and mass was first celebrated in West Haven in borough headquarters in the Thompson block. A cornerstone for the new brick church of St. Lawrence, at the corner of Main Street and Union Avenue, was laid in 1903. In 1917, the 12-room school was built. The parish also maintains a rectory and convent building.

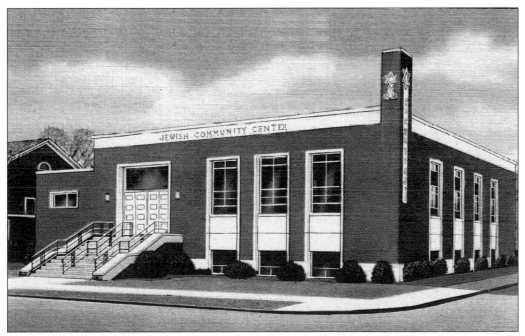

The Jewish Community Center on Washington Avenue was founded in 1928 on the property where the Seaside Male Seminary once stood. After a devastating fire, a new center was completed and dedicated in 1949 for religious, social, and educational purposes.

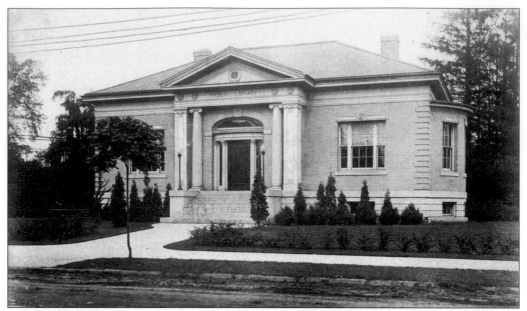

Through the efforts of the Village Improvement Association and a $10,000 gift from the Carnegie Foundation, the West Haven Public Library was opened to the public on September 1, 1909. The new building, located at the intersection of Campbell Avenue and Elm Street, housed 12,000 volumes.

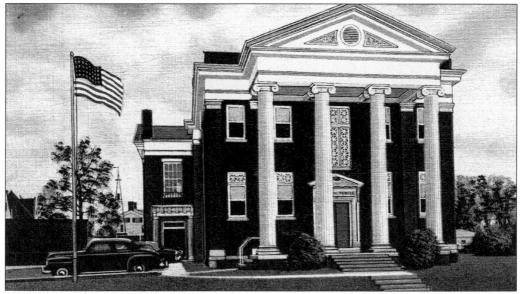

The town could boast of many active fraternal organizations, including the Masonic Order which first occupied its building on Center Street in 1913. The first meeting in the building was held by the Order of Eastern Star, according to the stated calendar. In 1923, the building was enlarged to the structure that stands today.

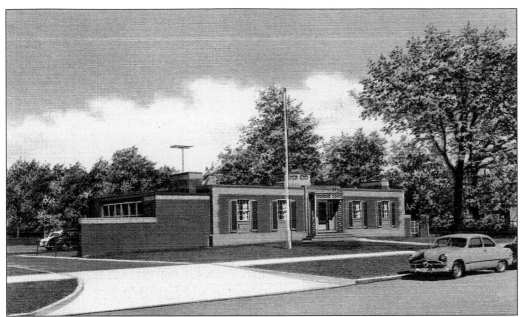

The West Haven Lodge 1537, Benevolent and Protective Order of Elks were instituted in August 1927. Early meetings were held in the Thompson School, but by 1936, the order was located in its present site.

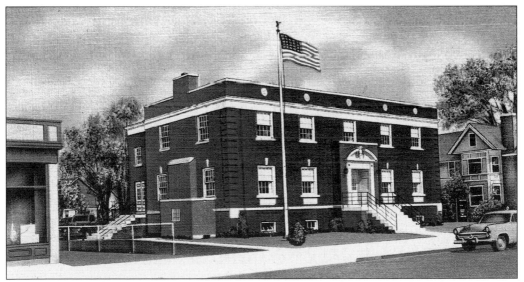

The Hughson-Miller Post No. 71, American Legion, has played an active role in the community from its founding in 1919. On June 25, 1950, the $80,000 building on Main Street was dedicated. The town donated $5,000 for a bronze plaque in the rotunda, honoring all West Haven veterans.

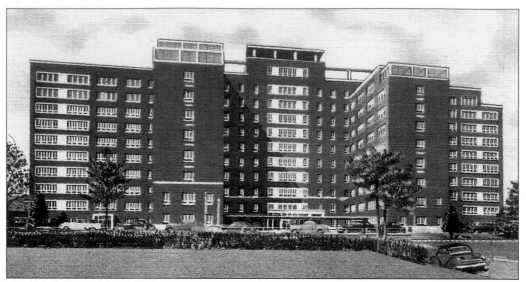

The Veteran's Administration Hospital, opened in 1953, is located on the grounds of the William Wirt Winchester Hospital for tuberculosis patients. The Campbell Avenue property called Lion Park was purchased by the New Haven Hospital Society for approximately $300,00 in 1911. During World War I, the government leased the hospital for tuberculosis patients and wounded soldiers. The entire project cost over $1 million at that time.

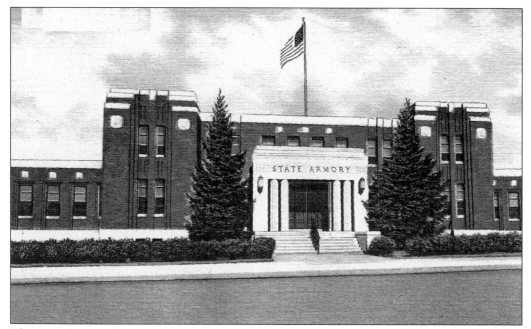

The West Haven Armory on Main Street was built by the State of Connecticut in 1932. It was considered by high-ranking military officials one of the finest buildings of its type. Many organizations held special events in the drill shed over the years.

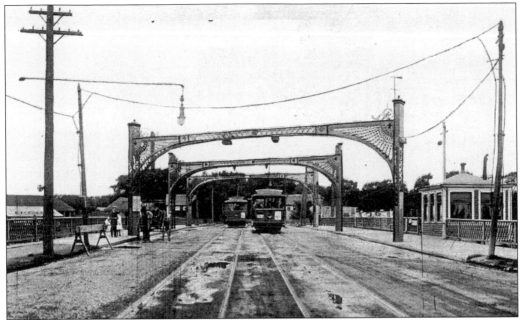

The busy electric trolley traveled regularly over the Kimberly Avenue drawbridge from New Haven en route to and from New Haven and Savin Rock.

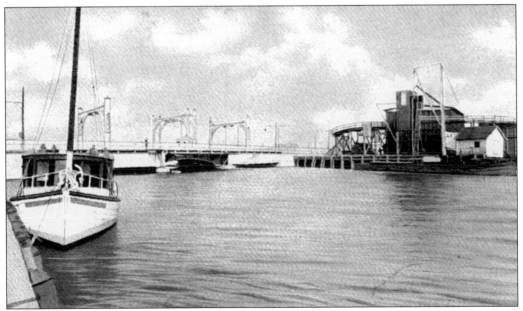

West Cove was a favorite mooring place for small boats that anchored on either side of the bridge or in the local boat yards.

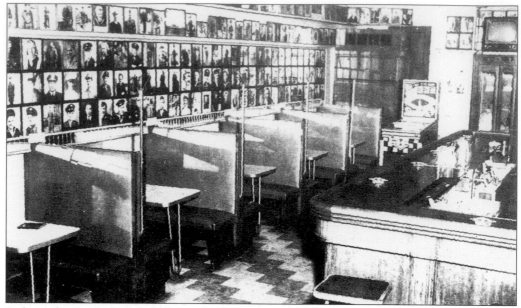

Perhaps the most popular place in town was Quigley's Restaurant on Campbell Avenue behind town hall. Walls were covered with pictures of every local serviceman and servicewoman.

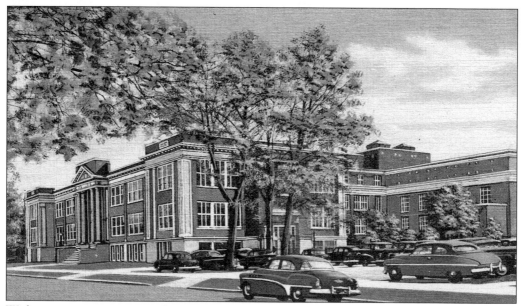

With an ever increasing population, it was necessary to build a new, modern, fully equipped high school with a capacity for 1,200 students, a four-year program, 38 classrooms, and a 1,300-seat auditorium. The school was completed and occupied in 1927.

Six

SCHOOLS,
LARGE AND SMALL

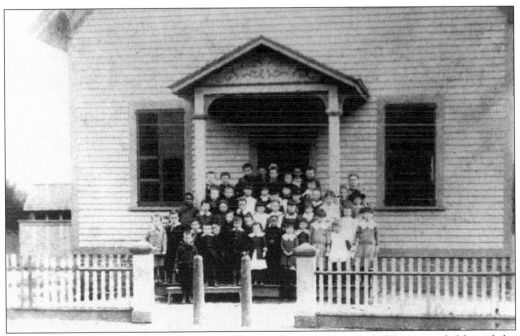

The founding fathers of West Farms insisted that education be provided for every child until the age of 16. The first record of a school on the West Haven Green was dated March 2, 1729. Many years later these students, in grades one through four, pose in front of the original two-room Union School on Center Street.

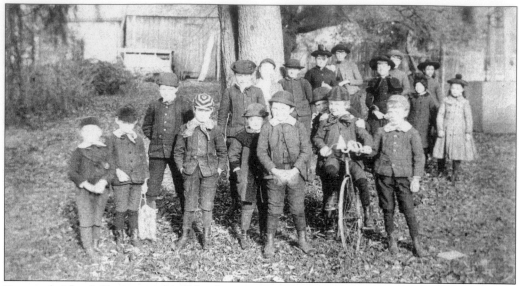

Boys and girls of all ages stand still for the cameraman around 1875.

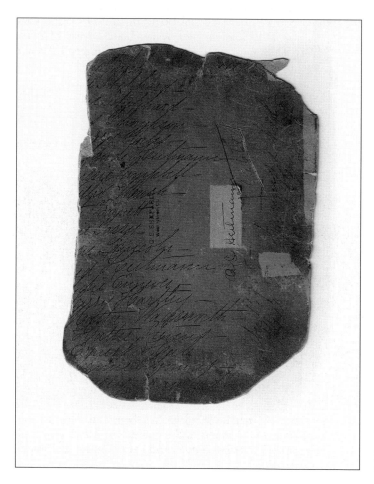

The names of many of the children are listed on the back of the photograph.

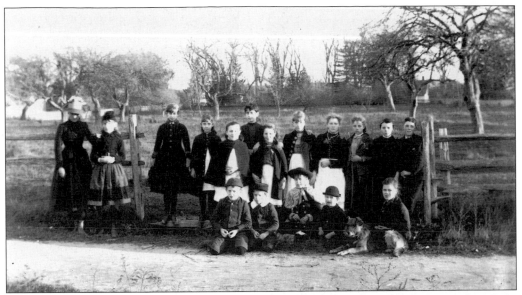

This group of public school students appears to be dressed for a special occasion around 1890. In the 18th and early 19th centuries, there were numerous schools in West Haven. Among them were the Seaside Male Seminary (Brown School), Commercial Boarding and Day School for Boys, Union School, Waldense School, Oak Hill Seminary for Young Ladies, Miss Marietta Sonage's School, Miss Phelps School, Miss Heitmann's School for Dames; Campbell Avenue School, Wood Street School, Lincoln School, and Thompson School.

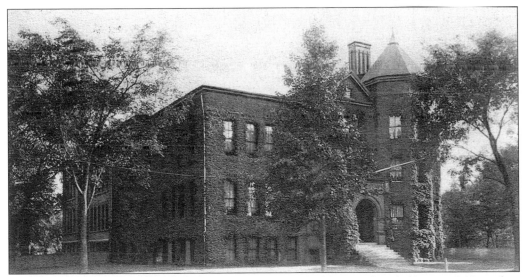

Union School progressed from a two-room wooden building with a belfry in 1860 to four classrooms and eventually—with the addition of 12 rooms and a tower—to a two-year high school. Students were responsible for their own textbooks, slates, and materials. School was in session year-round for many years after its opening.

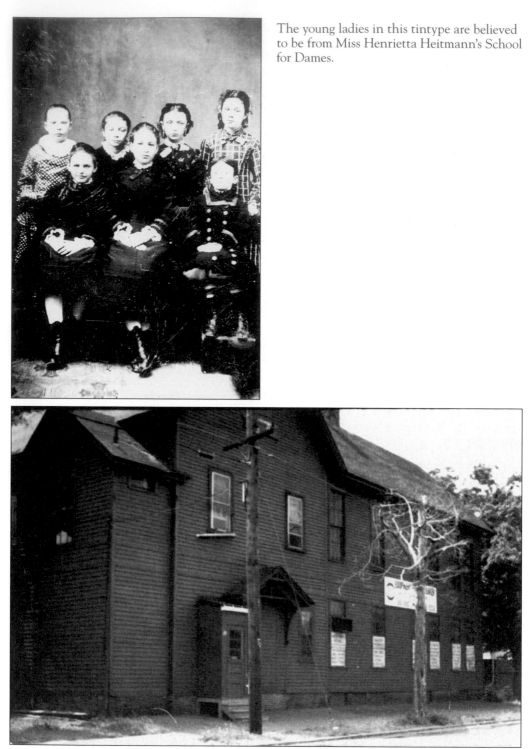

The young ladies in this tintype are believed to be from Miss Henrietta Heitmann's School for Dames.

West Haven school administrators and faculty of the old Wood Street School were the subjects of Newbery Award Winner Eleanor Estes's Moffit book series about the town of Cranberry. The building near Washington Avenue has undergone many conversions.

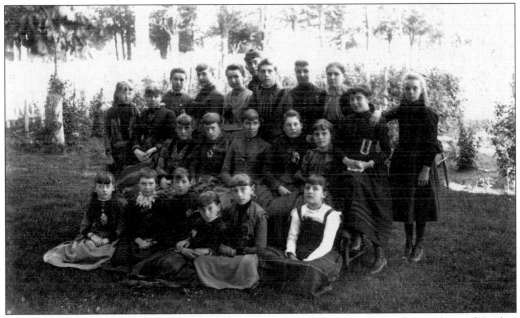

Written by Rollin Hine   Class 2nd

SPENCERIAN
System of Practical
Penmanship

In 12 Numbers, Four distinct Series,
by
P.R.SPENCER.

R.C.Spencer.
H.A.Spencer.
J.W.LUSK,
H.C.Spencer,
P.R.Spencer, Jun.,
L.P.Spencer,
M.D.L.Hayes.

NEW STANDARD EDITION.

J.B.Lippincott and Co.
Philadelphia.

NEW YORK
IVISON, BLAKEMAN, TAYLOR & Co.,
New York and Chicago.

Students were well versed in penmanship. This *Spencerian System of Practical Penmanship* copybook belonged to Rollin W. Hine. Many years later, on May 5, 1885, Hine was elected warden of the Borough of West Haven.

Young women from the private Oak Hill Seminary for Girls were under the tutelage of Sophie Northrup. The three-story building was located on Church Street, near Savin Avenue. The two upper stories were living quarters for the girls, some of whom came from great distances.

79

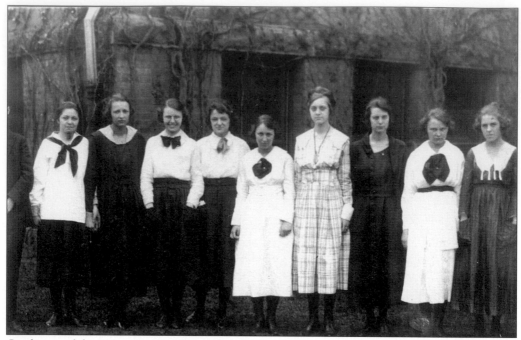

Graduates of the Union Street High School class of 1919 seem to have mixed emotions.

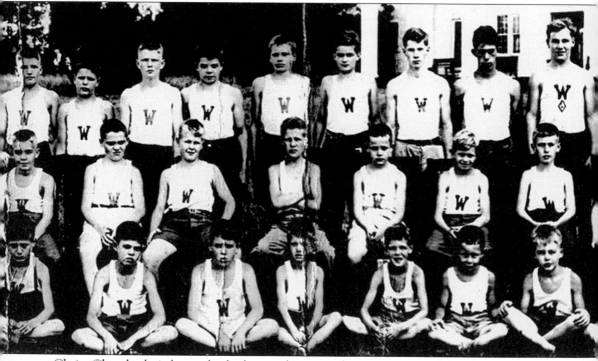

Christ Church choir boys who had exemplary attendance were rewarded with a two- to four-week stay at Camp Washington in Bantam Lake. The camp was established in 1917 by the

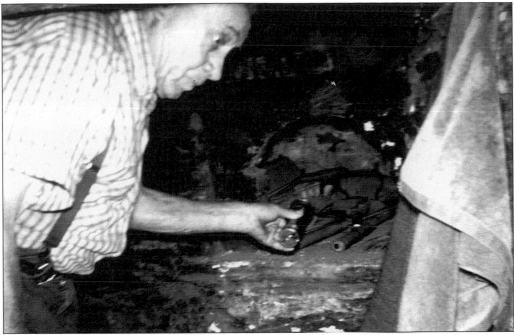

Educational field trips were always a treat, especially when they involved a tour of the historic Hubbard house by Clarence Hubbard, seen here.

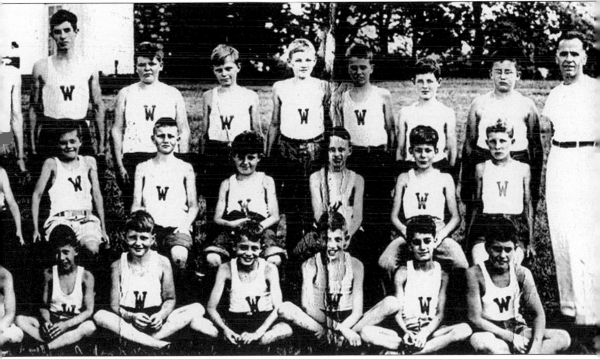

Reverend Floyd Steele Kenyon of West Haven.

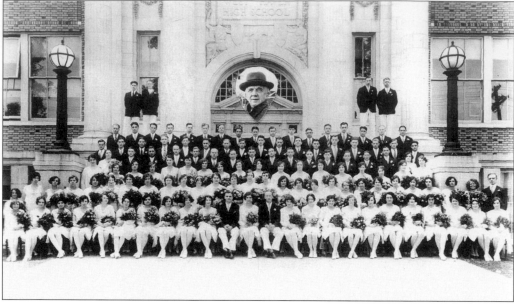

Six months before the stock market crashed, members of the West Haven High School class of 1929 sit for their senior picture, looking forward to a life "full of hope, ambition and carefree love."

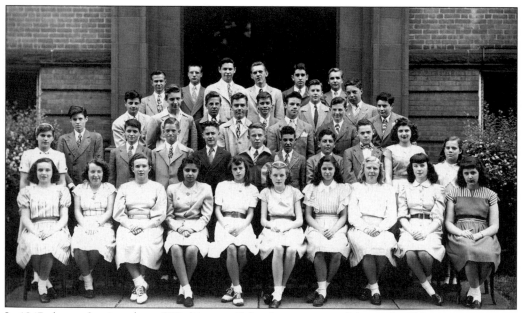

In 1947, the graduating class of Washington School prepares to celebrate the 300-year anniversary of the founding of the town.

Seven

SAVIN ROCK

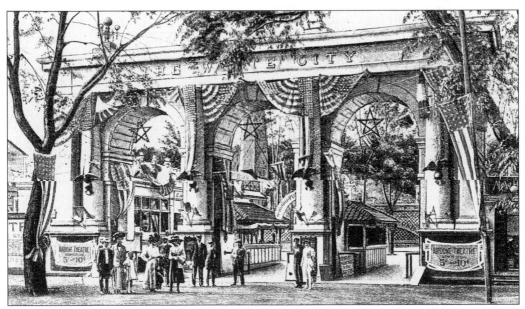

The enchanting arched entrance to White City at Savin Rock gives a hint of the excitement and pleasures of the park within.

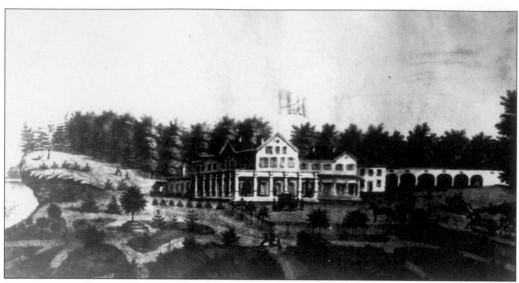

Perhaps the earliest hotel on the shore was the large, handsome, and inviting Savin Rock House, which sat next to the prominence covered with low-lying junipers that gave the area its name.

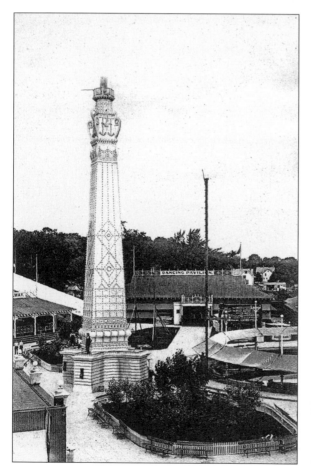

White City, a fully whitewashed Victorian amusement park, was created east of the Savin Rock. Genteel amusements surrounded the Electric Tower, an astonishing beacon with its thousands of brilliant light bulbs. The last surviving bulb is on exhibit at the Savin Rock Museum.

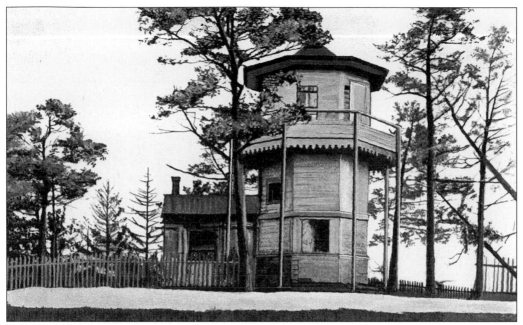

The 40-foot Savin Rock Observatory, which burned down in 1897, provided an unobstructed view from its perch at the top of the rise.

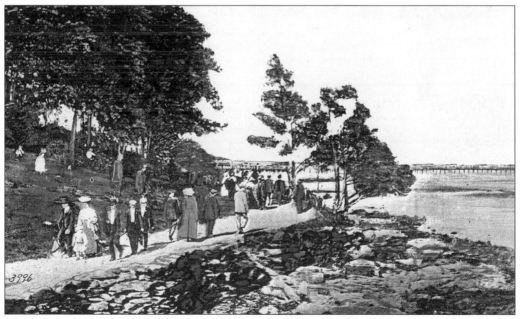

Thousands of visitors walked along Lover's Lane or sat on the rocks at the water's edge.

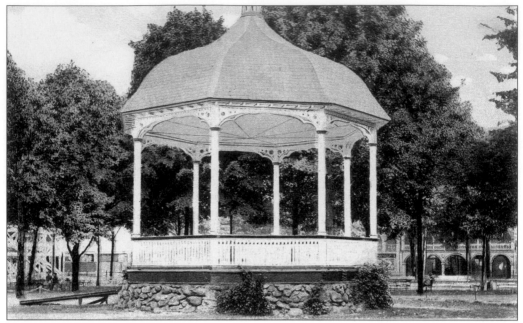

Entertainment in the bandstand included such favorites as John Philip Sousa and his marching band.

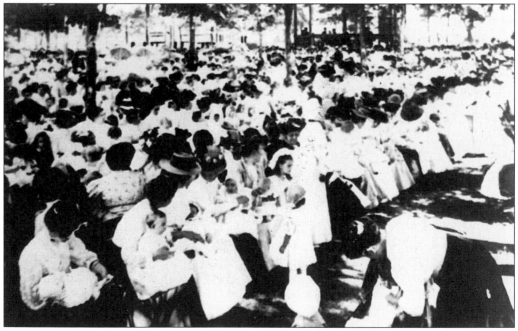

Hundreds of mothers brought their children to the Beautiful Baby Contest.

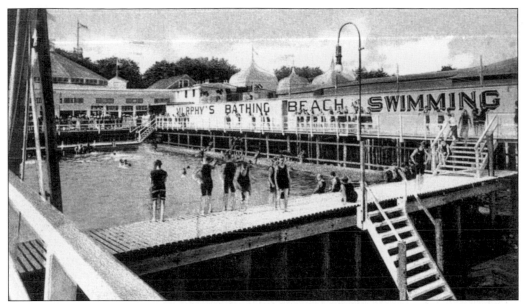

By 1912, bathers came from great distances to breathe in the salt air and swim in Murphy's Pool.

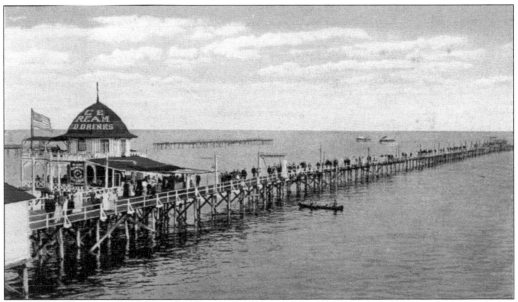

An ice cream cone or cool drink and a stroll on Wilcox's Long Pier provided a pleasant way to appreciate Long Island Sound. The pier was originally owned by George Kelsey. Then called Kelsey's Wharf, the pier was long enough to be used for practice by target excursions from New Haven, who found it to be the required distance for their sport.

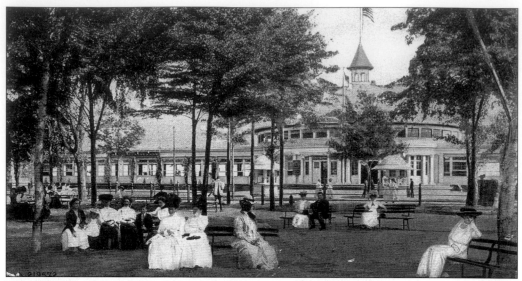

From 1903 to 1912, Bishop's Colonnade served sumptuous dinners in an elegant environment. Menus were hand painted on Japanese rice paper. In the etiquette of the day, a lady's menu would carry no price list.

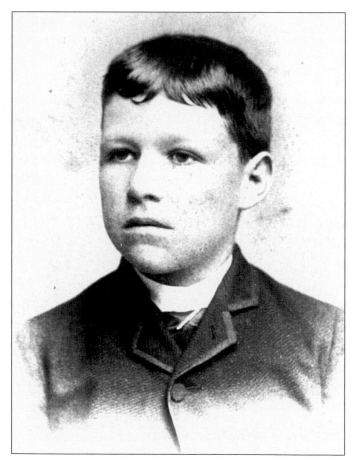

Young Yale Bishop sits for a proper portrait. It is said that his mother called him "Dot," as he weighed so little when he was born.

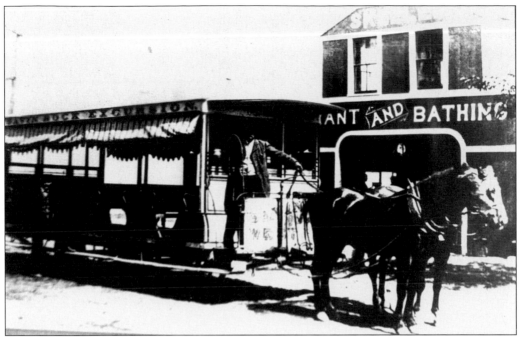

A horse-drawn Savin Rock excursion trolley provided transportation for those who wished to tour the park.

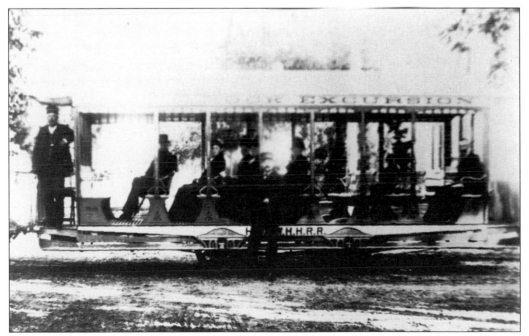

Savin Rock and the shore could be reached by taking the railroad's open-air electric trolley.

Newman's Ice Cream Parlors was known for its fine ice cream and candies, and of course, tobacco products for the gentlemen in 1900.

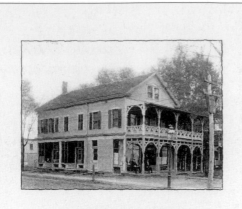

NEWMAN'S
ICE CREAM PARLORS

Beach and Grove Streets,
SAVIN ROCK.

Ice Cream, Soda, Confectionery, Cigars
and Tobacco.

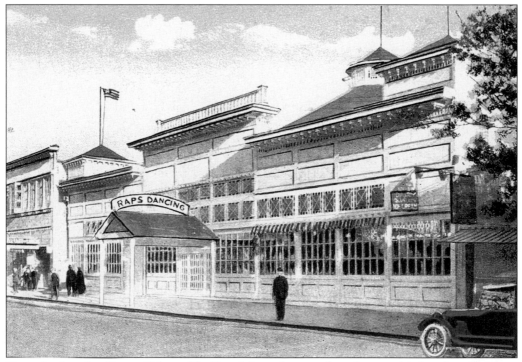

Over the decades, Dance Palaces like Rapp's brought marathon dancers, big bands, and singers like Frankie Laine.

The operators of the Roller-Boller Coaster posted their rules at its entrance.

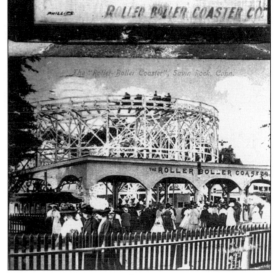

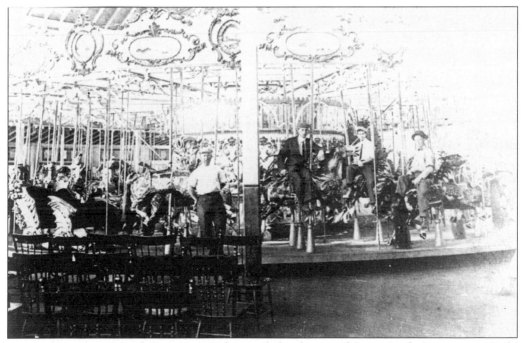

Carousels, such as Murphy's, were popular until the demise of Savin Rock Amusement Park, almost 100 years from its opening.

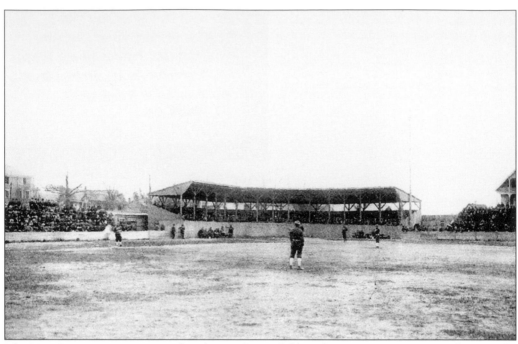

The New Haven League team played in its home field at the West Haven Base Ball Grounds. Old-timers always talked about the day that Babe Ruth and other greats came to town.

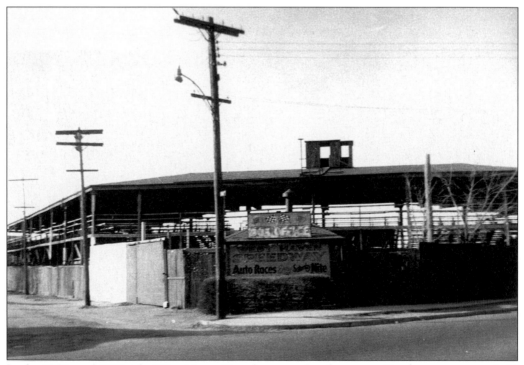

In the 1950s and 1960s, the West Haven Speedway was the place to go. Stock car races were held every Saturday night at 8:30, featuring top drivers from the United Stock Car Racing Club.

Eight

THE WESTERN SHORE

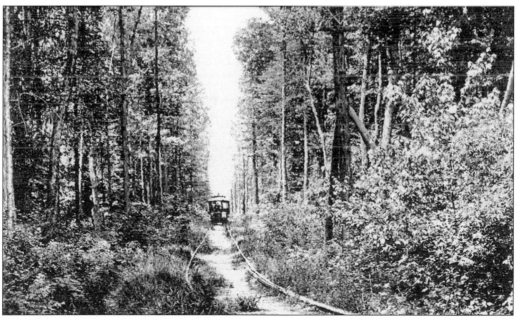

The electric trolley route expanded from Savin Rock westward, past Woody Crest, Prospect Beach, and Oyster River. The trolley ran parallel to the shoreline on an inland route.

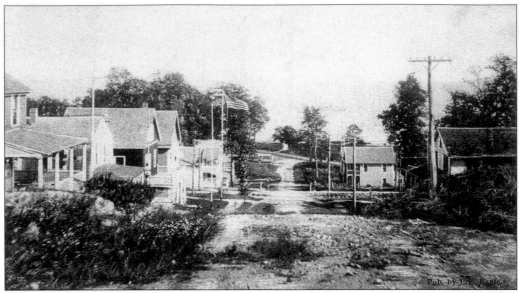

By 1915, Prospect Beach residents were used to seeing the electric trolley cross Dawson Avenue and Prospect Street at the top of the hill.

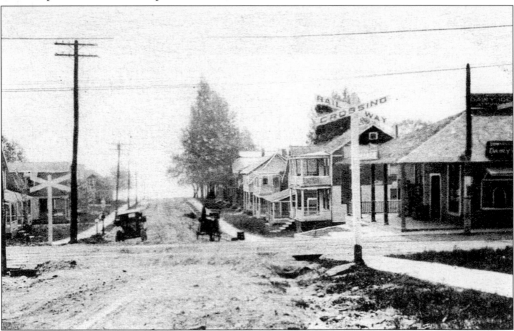

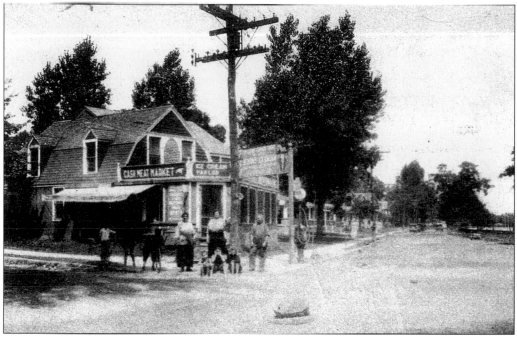

William's Meat Market, at the intersection of Ocean Avenue and Prospect Street, was one of many stores in Prospect Beach.

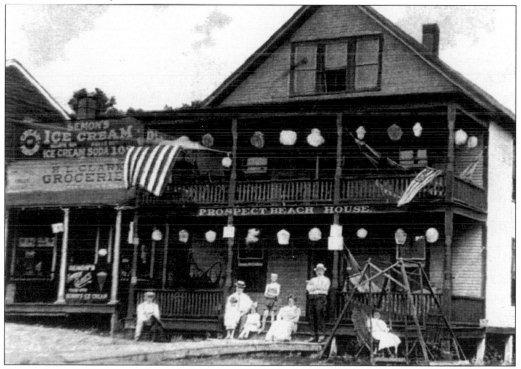

Flags adorn the Prospect Beach Inn in recognition of the Fourth of July. Japanese lanterns were traditionally lit for Illumination Night celebrations. In 1923, a yearly visitor wrote, "the place is pretty dead this year."

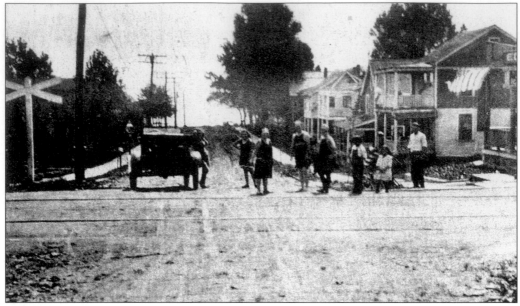

Whether on the hill or at a shoreline cottage, bathers had only as short walk to the beach.

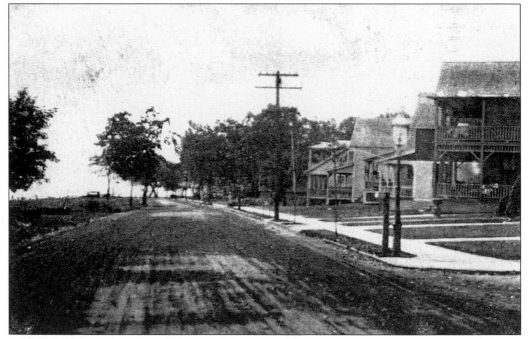

With the advent of the automobile, families were able to access summer cottages along Ocean Avenue westward to Oyster River.

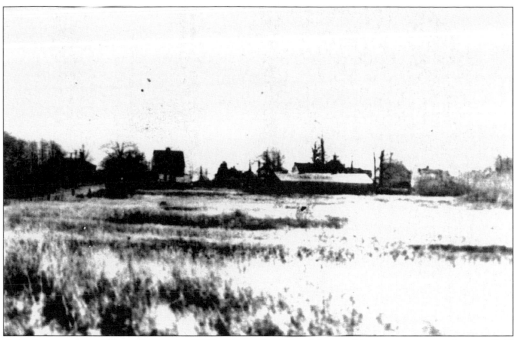

Aviation came to West Haven in 1925, when the West Haven Airport was created on a field located between Jones Hill Road, Annawon Avenue, South Street, and Ocean Avenue.

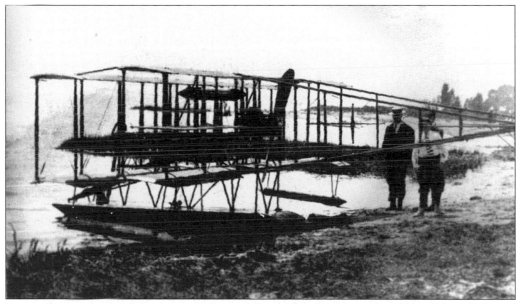

It was also not unusual to see a seaplane at Sandy Beach, Oyster River Bay. Pilots Jack and Charlie Tweed operated the business. An old memo notes that seaplanes and power craft were manufactured on Water Street in West Haven. Edward North, owner of the Hall Organ Company, was very interested in planes. He arranged a rather large air show for the Hughson American Legion Post, which ace pilot Eddie Rickenbacker attended. The airport attracted many important guests, among them Samuel O. Clark Jr., U.S. assistant attorney general. Clark was married to Charlotte Clark of the Northrup family.

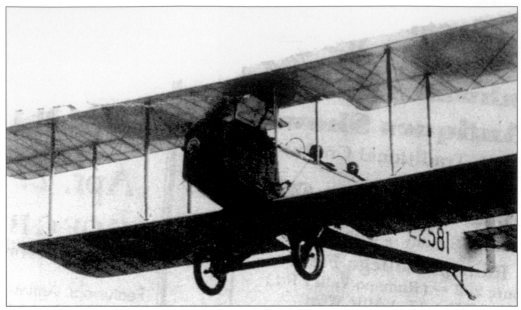

One could take a ride in a two-seater plane for $1.25. The trip went to Lighthouse Point, back over New Haven, past Sleeping Giant in Hamden, over Westville, and back to the airport.

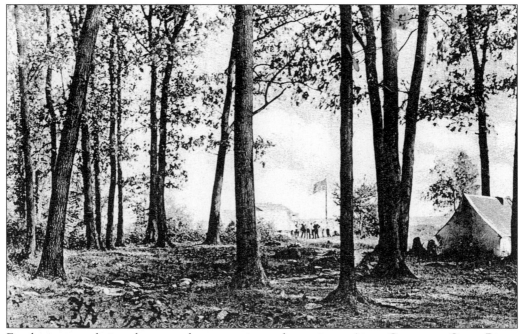

For those not so daring, there was always camping and canoeing at Aimes Grove near Oyster River.

Nine

OYSTER RIVER

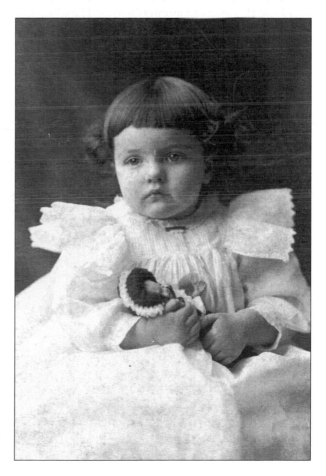

Pauline Atwell, daughter of the New York music store business owners, poses with her favorite doll.

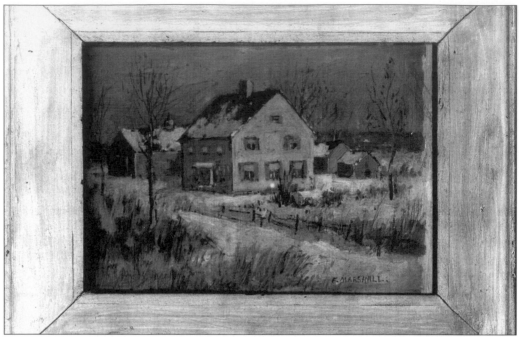

The 1700 Alfred Clark House, depicted in a 1942 painting by Frederick Marshall, was located at the southernmost point of Jones Hill Road, which terminated at the Oyster River Bay. Four oxen were used to bring an enormous hearthstone to the house, a showplace of its day.

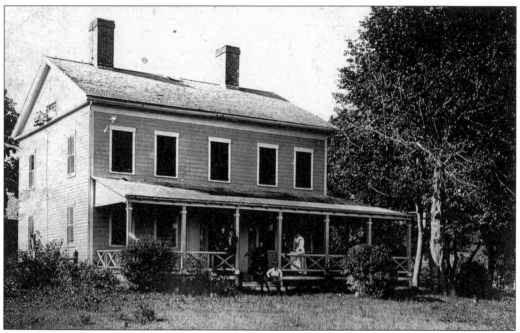

Jonas Fowler Merwin's first home in Oyster River boasted the largest walk-in fireplace in the region, with two Dutch ovens and an unprecedented double chimney. Merwin was the leading farmer in the region. All important meetings were held in his home. He owned flax fields and 18 to 21 flax wheels from which clothing was made.

To all People to whom these Presents shall come: GREETING.

KNOW YE, That I *Thomas Punderson of New Haven* in New Haven County & State of Connecticut for the Consideration of *Fifty three pounds Lawful Money* received to full Satisfaction of *Jonas Merwin of New Haven in New Haven* Do give, grant, bargain, sell, and confirm unto the said *Joseph Merwin &* to his Heirs & Assigns forever a certain lot or piece of land situated in New Haven in the parish of West Haven, containing nineteen tons and a quarter of land, & is bounded East & South on Highways. West on land of Asahel Thomas's wife. & North partly on land of Job Downs & partly on land of John Benham

To HAVE AND TO HOLD, the above granted and bargained Premises, with the Appurtenances thereof, unto *him* the said *Grantee his* Heirs and Assigns forever, to *his* and their own proper Use and Behoof. And also *I* the said *Grantor*

do for *my self & my* Heirs, Executors and Administrators, covenant with the said *Grantee his* Heirs and Assigns; that at and until the ensealing of these Presents *I am* well siezed of the Premises, as a good indefeasible Estate in Fee-simple, and have good Right to bargain and sell the same in Manner and Form as is above written, and that the same is free of all Incumbrances whatsoever. — AND FURTHERMORE, *I* the said *Grantor*

do by these Presents, bind *myself & my* Heirs forever to warrant and defend the above-granted and bargained Premises, to *him* the said *Grantee his*

Heirs and Assigns, against all Claims and Demands whatsoever. — IN WITNESS whereof *I* have hereunto set *my* Hand and Seal the *3d* Day of *June* Anno Domini 179 3

Signed, sealed and delivered
in the Presence of

Eliru Daggett
Henry Daggett

Thomas punderson

New Haven County New Haven June 3 Day A 1793
Personally appeared, *Cap Thomas Punderson* Signer and Sealer of the foregoing Instrument, and acknowledged the same to be his free Act and Deed, before me
Henry Daggett Jun Peace

N.B the Interlineation of these words be the same more or less were made before signing certified by me Henry Daggett Jus Peace

Jonas Merwin amassed approximately 390 acres in an area with abundant salt marsh, fishing, and good grazing. It was necessary to build a dike at the mouth of the Oyster River for the marshes. In order to do so, Merwin had to apply for permission from the federal government. His approval came from the office of George Washington, under the signature of aide Jonathan Trumbull. Trumbull later became governor of Connecticut.

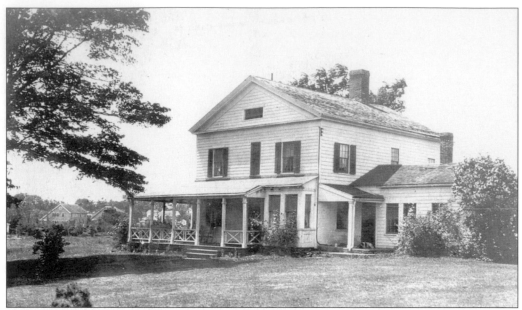

The second chimney of the Merwin house was sacrificed in 1890 to install a bathroom. In 1842, Sarah Jane Merwin married Jay Lord Northrup. The couple resided in the second family home, a 1780 house on Jones Hill Road.

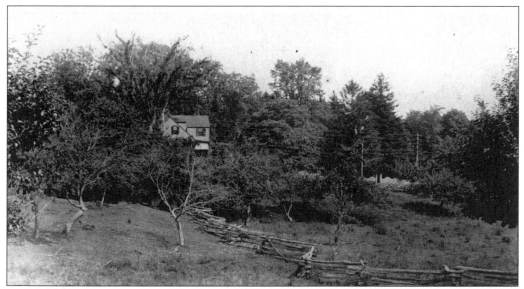

Clark, Atwell, Usher, Warner, Semon, Hubbard, Burwell, and Aimes were among the prominent families of the Oyster River area. Homes were built along or near Jones Hill Road, a key route to the center of the town. The Aimes property, on the eastern side of Jones Hill Road, could be seen from the neighboring Merwin-Northrup home.

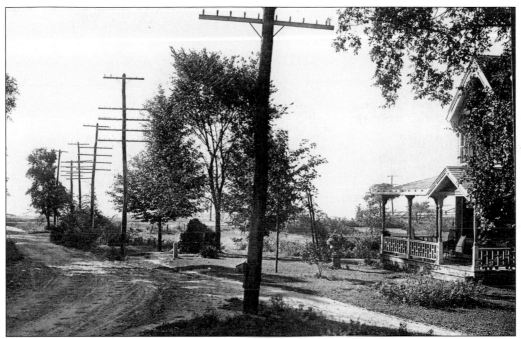

One had an unobstructed view of Oyster River Bay from the Usher House.

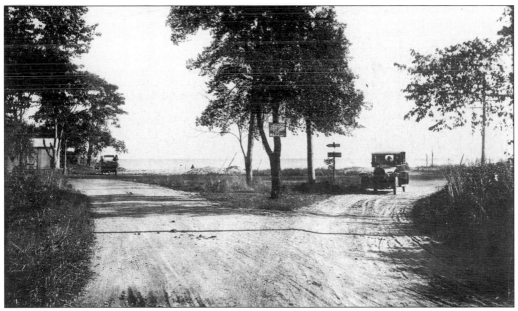

Jay Ansel Northrup cautiously approached the intersection of Jones Hill Road and Ocean Avenue. The posted sign reads, "Danger. Sound Klaxton."

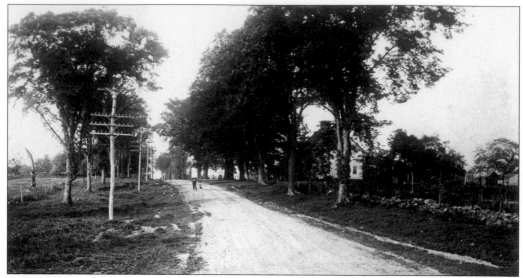

Young Arthur Warner stands with his dog on Jones Hill Road, between his home and the Hubbard property. He is near South Street (today) where there was once a toll station.

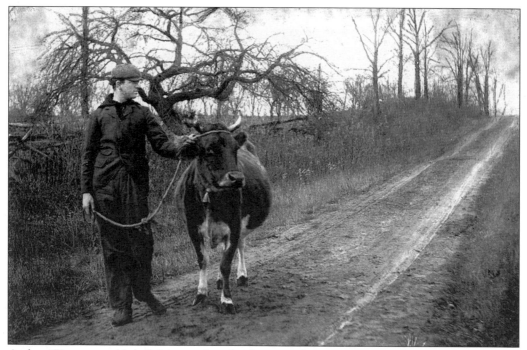

Arthur Warner would walk his cow from his home to the pasture on Benham Road.

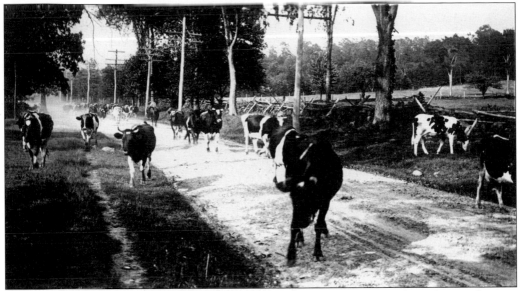

This herd of Northrup cows is heading for the barn at day's end. Hubbard Road is on the west and the Warner fields are on the right.

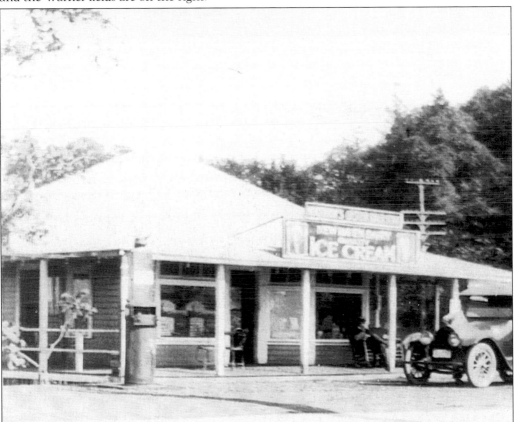

The area became popular with summer visitors. A favorite stop was the popular Northrup Ice Cream stand.

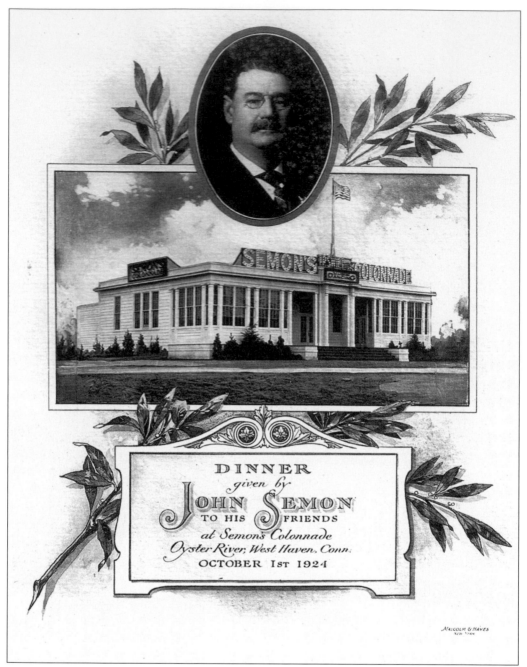

DINNER
given by
JOHN SEMON
TO HIS FRIENDS
at Semon's Colonnade
Oyster River, West Haven, Conn.
OCTOBER 1ST 1924

By the beginning of the 20th century, Oyster River attracted affluent families who built their summer cottages in the area. John Semon's Colonnade Restaurant attracted an elite clientele.

MENU

Hors d'Oeuvres

Cream of Fresh Mushrooms
Celery   Queen Olives   Salted Almonds

Kingfish Sauté Meuniere
Cucumbers

Filet Mignon Sauté Bonne Femme
Fresh Mushrooms   Green Peas
Potatoes Noisette   Onions Glace

Punch Romaine

Roast Pheasant
Salad Colonnade

Semon's Fancy Ice Cream
Petits Fours Glace

Cafe

Cigars
Cigarettes
White Rock
Ginger Ale

John Semon hosted a sumptuous seven-course dinner for friends on October 1, 1924.

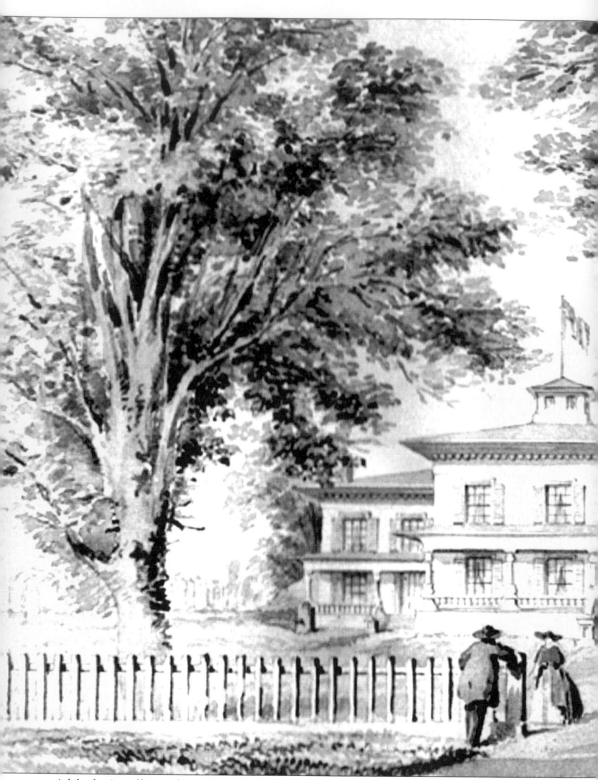

Adelaide Atwell's mother-in-law sketched the Elms during one of her visits there. The artist,

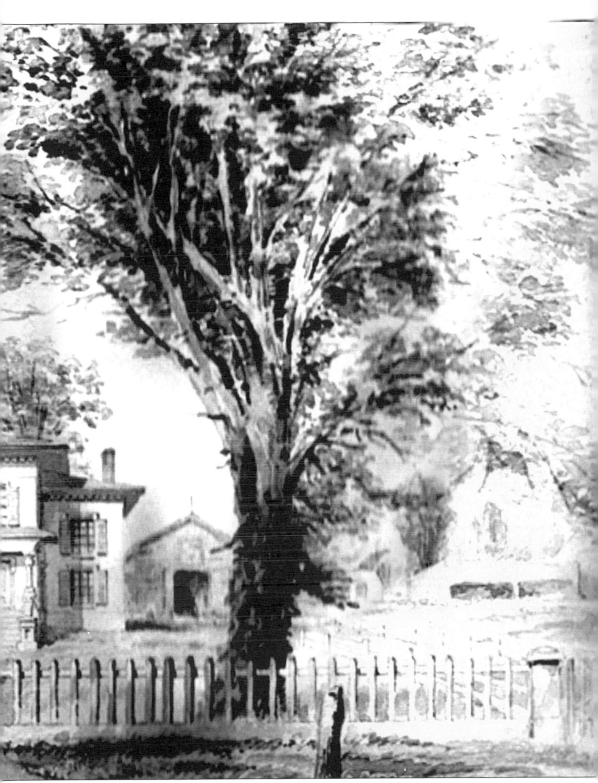

who would never sign her work, was known for her delicate, ethereal paintings.

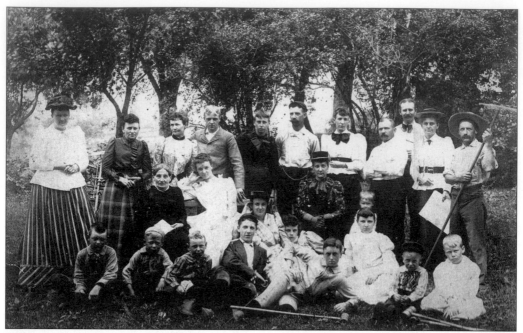

The Atwell family poses for a family portrait at the Elms. Among those pictured are Mary Adelaide Northrup (standing far left), sister of Jay Ansel Northrup; her mother-in-law, Mrs. Heyman Atwell (seated with a book); and Heidelberg-educated gentleman farmer George Atwell (far right, with his rake).

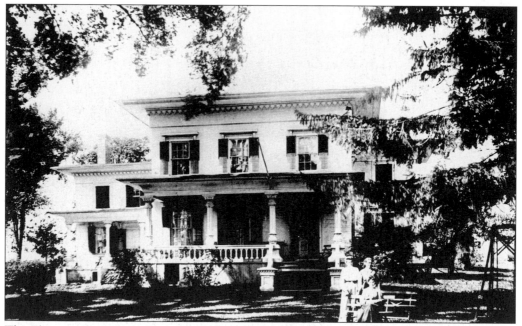

The Elms was built by a Captain Clark in 1859. The elegant porch columns were carved by Italian craftsmen. Paul Rolf George Atwell inherited the house from the second owner, his father, Heyman Atwell, owner of the Atwell Music Salon in New York City. Edith Northrup is the tall woman standing on the left.

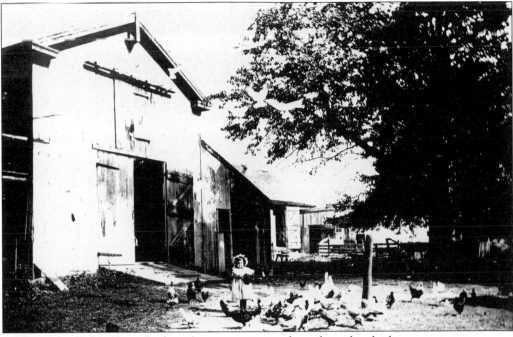

Pauline Atwell, for whom Pauline Avenue was named, tends to the chickens.

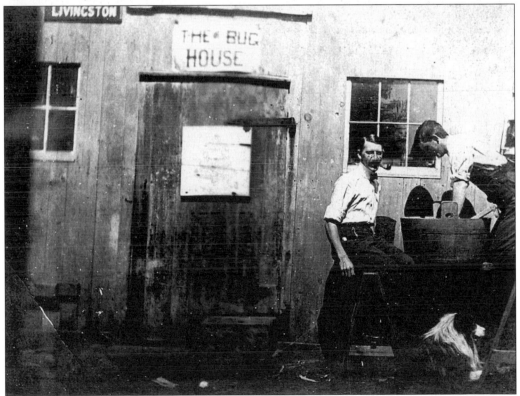

Guests with a sense of humor posted the sign that reads "The Bug House" over the entrance to the Atwell barn.

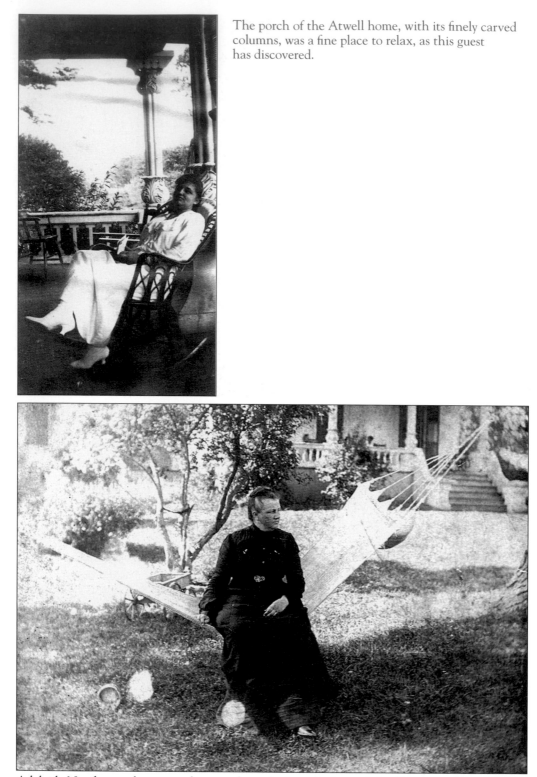

The porch of the Atwell home, with its finely carved columns, was a fine place to relax, as this guest has discovered.

Adelaide Northrup relaxes on a hammock on the lawn in front of the Elms.

112

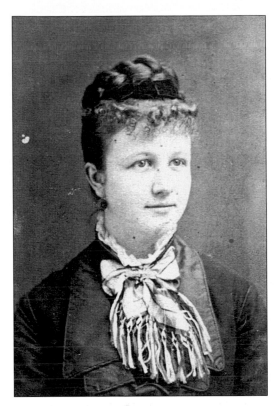

Paul Rolf George Atwell and his wife,
Adelaide, inherited the Elms from his father,
Heyman Atwell.

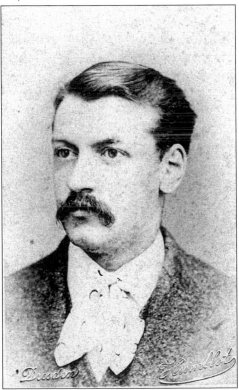

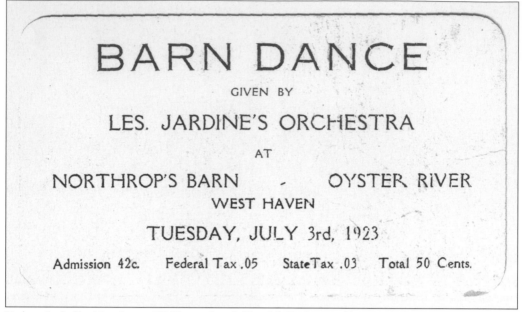

BARN DANCE

GIVEN BY

LES. JARDINE'S ORCHESTRA

AT

NORTHROP'S BARN - OYSTER RIVER
WEST HAVEN

TUESDAY, JULY 3rd, 1923

Admission 42c.   Federal Tax .05   State Tax .03   Total 50 Cents.

Esther Isabelle Northrup Wolfe, wife of Harold Ryder Wolfe, regularly hosted dances in Northrup's Barn, as evidenced by the admission ticket of July 3, 1923.

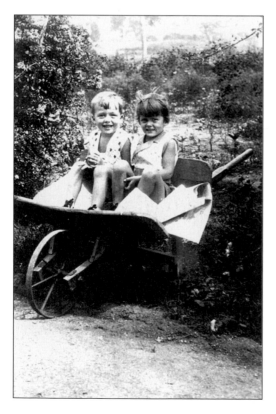

Twins Edward "Ted" and Margaret "Midge" Wolfe pose in the family wheelbarrow.

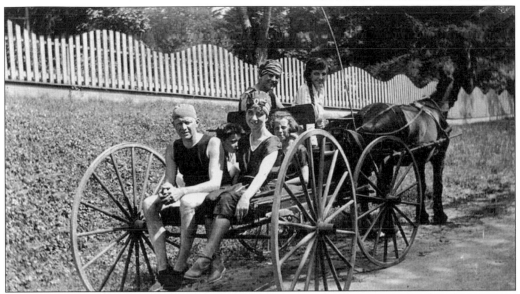

Pauline Atwell (far right) and friends head south on Jones Hill Road to the beach at Oyster River Bay.

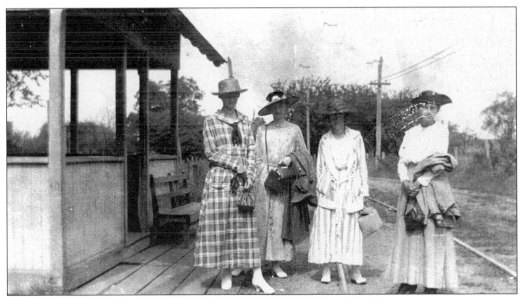

Ladies await the trolley at the Oyster River Station.

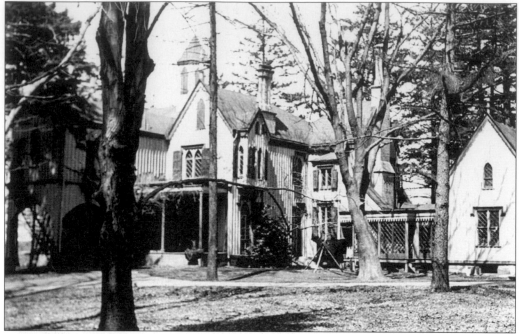

Martinstowe was the home of Dr. John Martin Aimes. This spacious and elegant mansion house, built high on the bluff, had servants' quarters, a library, a carriage drive-through, and a tower. Son Hubert Aimes, born in 1876, and grandson Peter Martin Aimes also lived there.

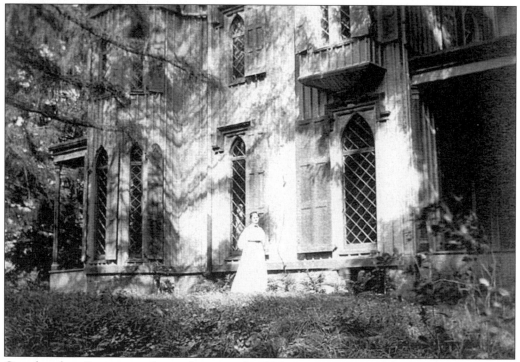

Grandmother Sorgen stands on the grounds of Martinstowe, owned by her daughter Eloise Sorgen Aimes and son-in-law Hubert Aimes.

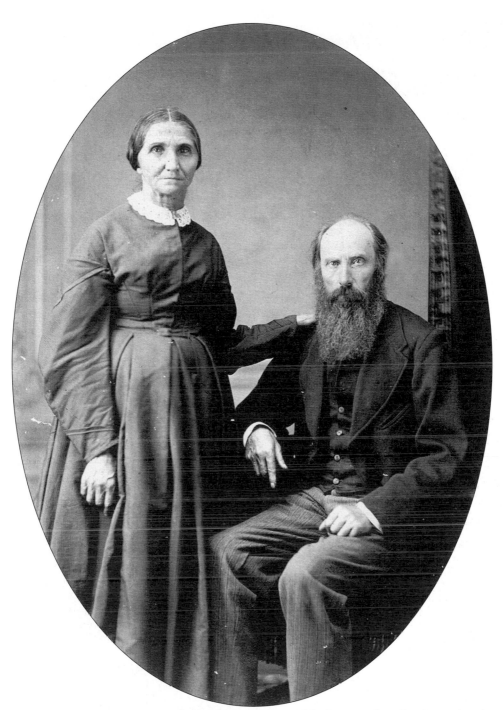

Dr. and Mrs. John Martin Aimes built Martinstowe in 1851. Prior to that, Dr. Aimes lived in a home at the northwest corner of Main Street and Savin Avenue. He inherited that house from his grandmother Elizabeth Blyer, who died on September 9, 1881.

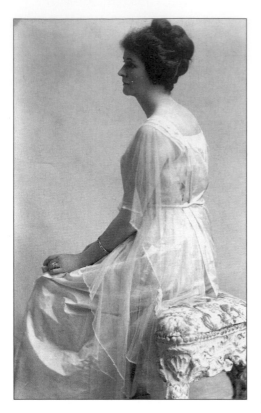

Hubert and Eloise Aimes were the second-generation owners of Martinstowe.

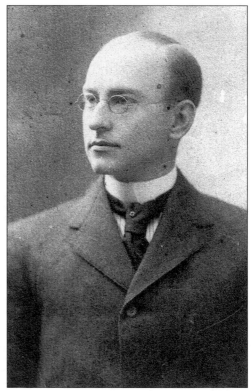

Climbing the horse block was no challenge to young Peter Martin Aimes.

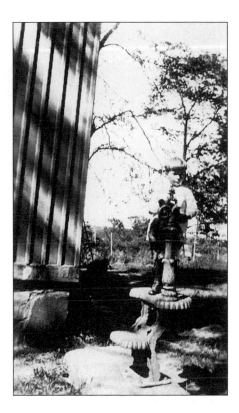

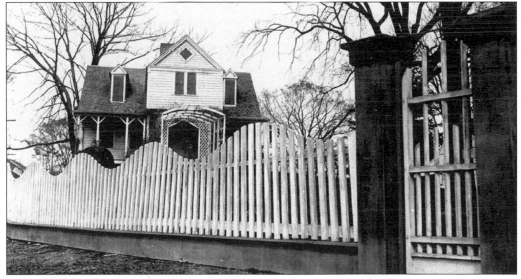

The Bellevedere Gate to the Hubert Aimes property was a landmark of a sort.

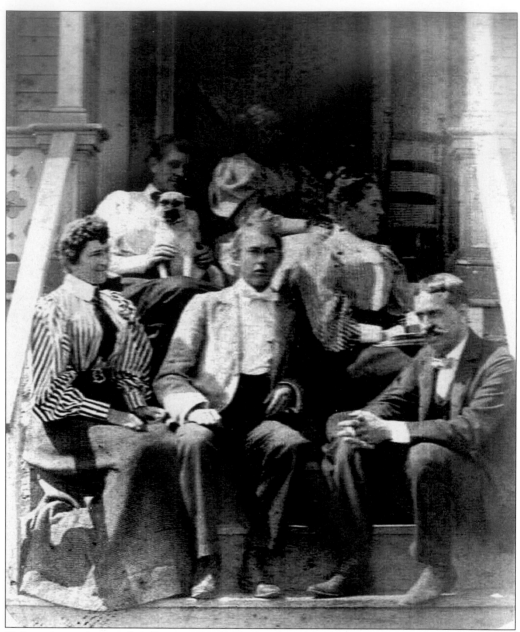

Hubert Aimes (center front) is surrounded by his friends. Clockwise from bottom left are Mrs. Kingsley, Henrietta (Aunt "Sis") Heitmann holding dog Peter, Mary Hungerford, Aunt Fannie Heitmann, and Harry Hungerford.

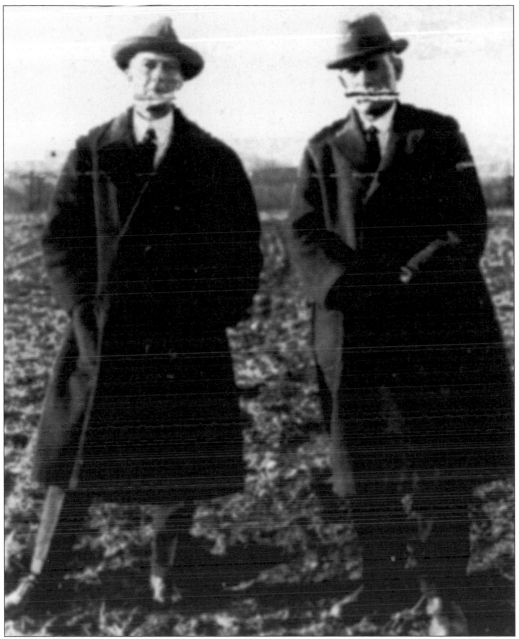

In 1922, C. E. Thompson (left), hired noted golf course designer Willie Park to create a state-of-the-art 18-hole course for the new country club at Elm Terrace. The club was a recreation center, with banquet and dance halls. Annual fees ranged from $25 to $100.

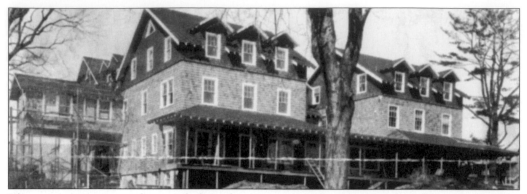

The construction was a huge task, but when it was completed there was nothing like the Elm Terrace Country Club in the entire region.

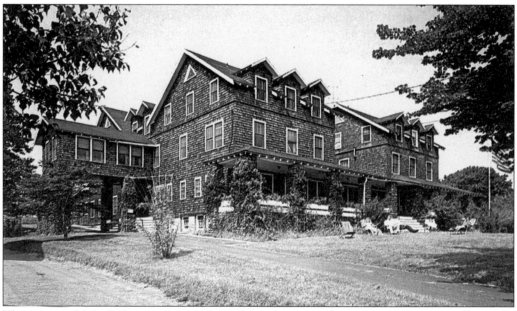

The country club had 65 guest rooms with telephones, a tearoom, a pro shop, and accommodations for every sport imaginable. Should one prefer, there were several private guest cottages on the grounds.

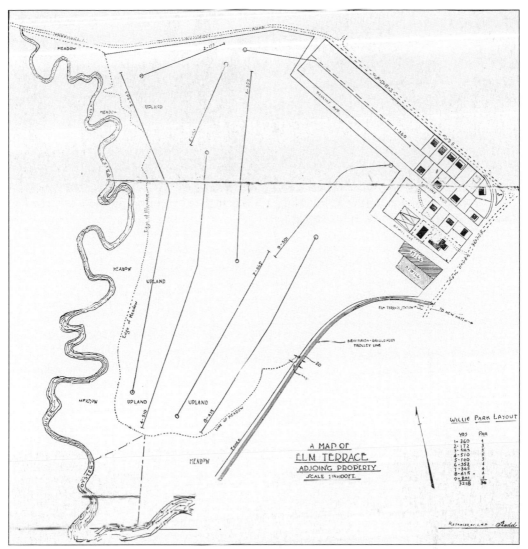

This map from the advertising brochure shows the layout of the main building and the guest houses, which still stand on Pauline Avenue and Woodmont Road.

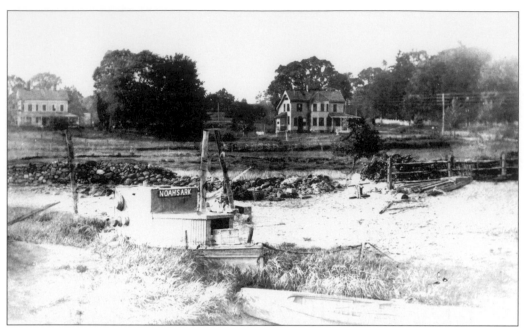

Local character Bill Clinton relaxes aboard his boat *Noah's Ark*. The Merwin-Northrup home is on the left in the rear, and the Usher house on the right. Northrup built the latter home for his sister Adella Usher.

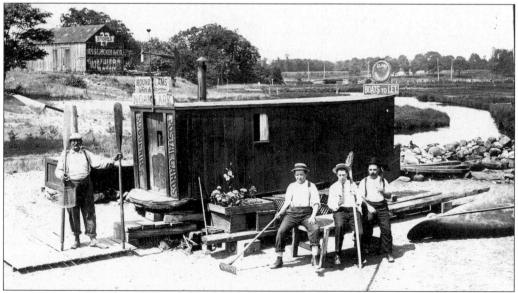

Bill Clinton located his entrepreneurial business on the West Haven side of the Oyster River. He sold postcards, round clams, and souvenirs and had boats to let. The trolley bridge to Milford is visible in the background. The barn belonged to Homer Swift, who built and maintained the first dike.

Ten

WEST HAVEN
HISTORICAL SOCIETY,
THEN AND NOW

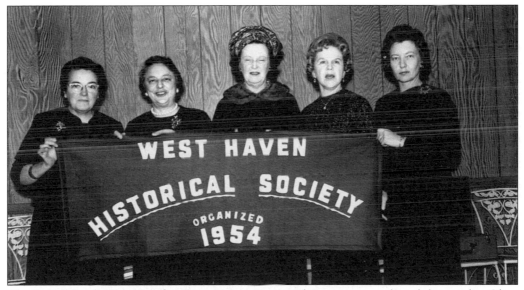

The first elected officers of the West Haven Historical Society were, from left to right, Olive Kerr, Harriet North, Marie Reilly, Gladys Treanor, and Lee Cobb. The society was organized in 1954, after several community leaders realized that there was a need to discover, procure, and preserve facts and materials having general historic value and particular to the history of West Haven. The society has taken responsibility for the identification, preservation, and marking of historic sites and landmarks and for educational and promotional programs. Membership is open to anyone with an interest in history.

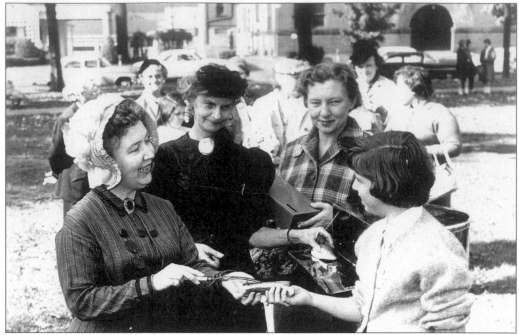

Members conduct monthly meetings, educational trips, and school lectures and demonstrations. In addition, in costume, they raise funds with activities such as this food and white elephant sale on the Green on October 17, 1979.

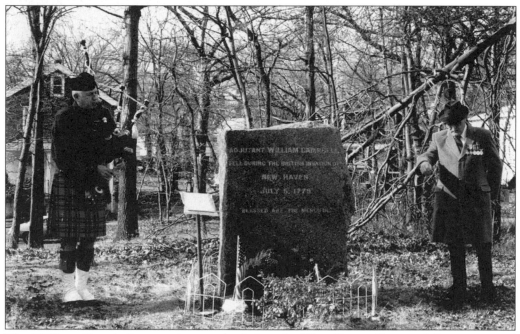

The William Campbell grave site was deeded to the West Haven Historical Society around the time of the nation's bicentennial celebration. A bagpiper mourns the death of Adjutant Campbell, setting the stage for a solemn ceremony at his monument.

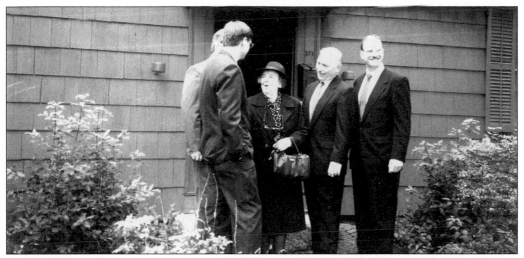

Dignitaries visit the Ward-Heitmann House after a mortgage has been secured for the purchase of the property from the National Trust for Historic Preservation. From left to right are Mayor H. Richard Borer, assistant Douglas Cutler, historical society president Harriet North, Lafayette Bank president Raymond Peach, and attorney Joseph Rini. In 1995, the society donated an initial $10,000 with the understanding that a second building would eventually be erected to be used by both organizations to house articles and artifacts and to provide orientation, education, and meeting space. The Museum Foundation was created by Carole A. Laydon McElrath and former educator Jeffrey M. Reilly, son of the society's first president. Nancy Ciarleglio, Ginny Reinhart, and Cutler completed the original feasibility survey committee.

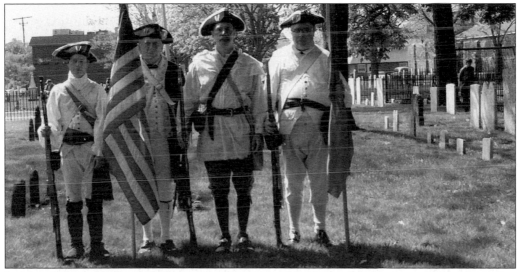

In May 2004, members of the Connecticut Society of the Sons of the American Revolution, Eve Lear Chapter of the Daughters of the American Revolution, and the 2nd Company Governor's Foot Guard joined the historical society in a solemn ceremony during which the graves of 19 Revolutionary War patriots were marked. The event celebrated the restoration of the Old Burial Grounds by the society. City dignitaries, Sponsors of Stones, and the public participated in two days of civic and religious activities. A Founders' Day stone was dedicated by the Congregational church and a concert was held in Christ Church. Churchgoers in Colonial dress were drummed to both churches. The project was made possible through a grant from the City of West Haven.

127

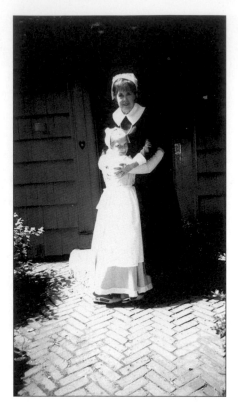

Historical society officer Mary Lee Neale and granddaughter Brittany Carew are typical of members who volunteer at local history-oriented museums as docents, historical trolley tour guides, reenactors, and participants in special events.

Historical society secretary Betty Roy gives her undivided attention as Henry Townshend shares information about Raynham, his family home. The officers of the historical society sponsored Raynham, and the society provided trained docents for the 2005 East Shore House Tour to benefit the Fort Nathan Hale Restoration Association.